Ultrean Air Fryer Cookbook for Beginners

1000-Day Crispy, Easy & Fresh Recipes to Fry, Bake, Grill, and Roast with Your Ultrean Air Fryer

Sarally Crain

© Copyright 2021 Sarally Crain - All Rights Reserved.

In no way is it legal to reproduce, duplicate, or transmit any part of this document by either electronic means or in printed format. Recording of this publication is strictly prohibited, and any storage of this material is not allowed unless with written permission from the publisher. All rights reserved.

The information provided herein is stated to be truthful and consistent, in that any liability, regarding inattention or otherwise, by any usage or abuse of any policies, processes, or directions contained within is the solitary and complete responsibility of the recipient reader. Under no circumstances will any legal liability or blame be held against the publisher for any reparation, damages, or monetary loss due to the information herein, either directly or indirectly.

Respective authors own all copyrights not held by the publisher.

Legal Notice:

This book is copyright protected. This is only for personal use. You cannot amend, distribute, sell, use, quote or paraphrase any part of the content within this book without the consent of the author or copyright owner. Legal action will be pursued if this is breached.

Disclaimer Notice:

Please note the information contained within this document is for educational and entertainment purposes only. Every attempt has been made to provide accurate, up-to-date and reliable, complete information. No warranties of any kind are expressed or implied. Readers acknowledge that the author is not engaging in the rendering of legal, financial, medical or professional advice.

By reading this document, the reader agrees that under no circumstances are we responsible for any losses, direct or indirect, which are incurred as a result of the use of information contained within this document, including, but not limited to, errors, omissions, or inaccuracies.

Table of Contents

Introduction 5
Chapter 1: Ultrean Air Fryer Basics 6
   What is Ultrean Air Fryer? 6
   How does the Ultrean Air Fryer Works?
   6
   Structure of the Ultrean Air Fryer 8
   Benefits of Using Ultrean Air fryer 8
   Cleaning and Maintenance 10
Chapter 2: Breakfast 11
   Savory & Crispy Hash Browns 11
   Sweet Potato with Cranberries 12
   Cheese Omelet 13
   Zucchini Egg Muffins 14
   Greek Egg Muffins 15
   Crispy Breakfast Potatoes 16
   Herb Egg Breakfast Muffins 17
   Cheese Egg Bake 18
   Italian Egg Muffins 19
   Kale Egg Muffins 20
Chapter 3: Poultry Recipes 21
   Juicy Turkey Breast 21
   Crispy Chicken Wings 22
   Flavorful Lemon Pepper Wings 23
   Meatballs 24
   Flavorful Chicken Fajitas 25
   Easy BBQ Chicken 26
   Juicy Turkey Patties 27
   Quick Chicken Patties 28
   Cajun Chicken Nuggets 29
   Healthy Greek Chicken 30
   Sesame Chicken 31
   Buffalo Meatballs 32
   Jerk Chicken Wings 33
   Crispy Chicken Drumsticks 34
   Tender & Flavorful Chicken Breast ... 35
   Juicy & Tasty Chicken Tenders 36
   Easy Turkey Burger Patties 37
   Turkey Meatballs 38
   Meatballs 39
   Asian Chicken Patties 40
   Cajun Chicken Thighs 41
   Greek Meatballs 42
   Simple Adobo Chicken 43
   Mustard Chicken Tenders 44
   Crispy Chicken Breast 45
Chapter 4: Beef, Pork & Lamb 46
   Simple & Juicy Pork Chops 46
   Sweet & Spicy Pork Chops 47
   Mexican Meatballs 48
   Meatballs 49
   Juicy Pork Chops 50
   Meatballs 51
   Delicious Steak Fajitas 52
   Air Fryer Perfect Steak 53
   Steak Bites 54
   Sweet & Juicy Pork Chops 55
   Flavorful Steak Bites 56
   Tender & Juicy Pork Chops 57
   Marinated Pork Chops 58
   Brined Pork Chops 59
   Asian Meatballs 60
   Dijon Lamb Chops 61
   Baked Meatballs 62
   Meatballs 63
   Air Fryer Pork Ribs 64
   Simple & Delicious Pork Chops 65
Chapter 5: Fish & Seafood 66
   Delicious Shrimp 66

Delicious Crab Patties..................... 67	**Chapter 7: Snack & Appetizers 101**
Juicy & Flaky Salmon 68	Healthy Chicken Meatballs 101
Quick & Juicy Tilapia 69	Crispy Potato Wedges...................... 102
Quick & Spicy Scallops 70	Delicious BBQ Chickpeas 103
Flavors Blackened Salmon 71	Delicious Broccoli Tots 104
Asian Salmon 72	Crispy Apple Fries 105
Moist & Crisp Cod 73	Easy Carrot Fries.............................. 106
Asian Shrimp 74	Sweet Cinnamon Chickpeas 107
Lemon Butter Cod............................ 75	Crispy Veggies.................................. 108
Crispy Salmon Patties 76	Air Fryer Pecans............................... 109
Spicy Salmon Fillets 77	Rosemary Basil Mushrooms 110
Lemon Pepper White Fish Fillets....... 78	Savory & Healthy Almonds............. 111
Marinated Asian Salmon 79	Crispy Eggplant Slices...................... 112
Curried Cod...................................... 80	Healthy Turkey Patties..................... 113
Easy Teriyaki Salmon 81	Cripsy Chicken Wings...................... 114
Asian Sweet & Spicy Salmon............. 82	Tasty Chicken Patties 115
Quick Rosemary Shrimp.................... 83	Crispy Chicken Nuggets 116
Lemon Garlic Spicy Shrimp 84	Tasty Chicken Tenders 117
Flavorful Shrimp Fajitas..................... 85	Crispy Burger Patties 118
Chapter 6: Vegetable & Side Dishes........ 86	Tasty Eggplant Chunks..................... 119
Sweet Potato Bites............................ 86	Flavorful Okra................................... 120
Spicy Brussel Sprouts 87	**Chapter 8: Desserts 121**
Crispy Sugar Snap Peas..................... 88	Moist Banana Muffins 121
Perfect Green Beans......................... 89	Chocolate Cake 122
Mushroom with Beans & Onions...... 90	Easy Apple Crisp.............................. 123
Tasty Butternut Squash 91	Peanut Butter Cookies..................... 124
Simple Mexican Potatoes 92	Choco Chip Cookies 125
Rosemary Potatoes 93	Cinnamon Bagel Bites...................... 126
Tasty Cauliflower Florets 94	Chocolate Donuts............................ 127
Garlic Cauliflower Florets 95	Brownie Muffins.............................. 128
Simple Sweet Potato Fries 96	Almond Flour Muffins 129
Healthy Zucchini Patties 97	Lemon Muffins 130
Air Fryer Potatoes & Carrots............. 98	**Chapter 9: 30-Day Meal Plan 131**
Broccoli Fritters................................ 99	**Conclusion 134**
Tasty Zucchini & Squash................... 100	

Introduction

The Ultrean air fryer is the all in one cooking appliances available in the market. It is a versatile cooking device capable to perform different cooking tasks like air fry, roasting, grilling, and baking into single cooking appliances. You never need to purchase a separate appliance for each function. The Ultrean air fryer is very simple to use anyone can easily operate this appliance. It is capable to cook almost all types of healthy and delicious dishes. The air fryer comes with a 4-quart cooking capacity which is large enough for a small family to cook their daily meal.

The Ultrean air fryer uses rapid hot air circulation techniques to cook your food faster and evenly. Using this technique you can air fry French fries, chicken wings, potato chips, mozzarella sticks and more. It makes your food nice moist from inside and makes crunchy from outside. It also gives nice brown texture over your food. The Ultrean air fryer is one of the healthy methods of cooking your food with fewer fats and oils. Less fat and oils mean less calorie intake and the food cooks into air fryer maintains the nutritional values in the food.

This cookbook contains healthy and delicious air fried recipes comes from different categories like breakfast, poultry, beef, lamb, pork, seafood, fish, vegetables, side dishes, appetizers, snacks, and desserts. The recipes written in this book are unique and written into an easily understandable form. All the recipes start with their preparation and cooking time followed by step by step cooking instructions. Each recipe written in this cookbook ends with their nutritional value information. The nutritional value information will help to keep track of daily calorie consumptions. The book ends with 30 days meal plan. There are few books available in the market on this topic thanks for choosing my cookbook. I hope you love and enjoy all the recipes written in this cookbook.

Chapter 1: Ultrean Air Fryer Basics

What is Ultrean Air Fryer?

The Ultrean Air Fryer is advanced air fryer comes into a compact size with LCD and operating buttons. It is one of the multifunctional air fryers not only used for air frying your food but also performs different cooking operations like grilling, roasting and baking your favourite food. The air fryer comes with oval shape design and works on 1500 watts power and capable to produce 400°F temperature to cook your food faster. It comes with 4-quart cooking capacity and large enough to cook small family food. Ultrean air fryer cooks your food into very less oil or sometimes no oil. A bowl of French fries needs just a tablespoon or less oil to air fry your food without changing the taste and texture like deep-fried food.

The Ultrean Air Fryer works on an innovative and advanced rapid air circulation technology to heat-up your oven rapidly. It circulates very hot air (400° F) into the cooking chamber to air fry your food faster and evenly. The heating elements and convection fan is attached at the top of the cooking chamber. The air fryer convection fan blows hot air and equally distribute into the cooking chamber to get even cooking results every time. The Ultrean air fryer is easy to operate and having round shape LCD with easy to operate buttons. The air fryer has an auto switch off timer works between 0 to 30 minutes and you can adjust the cooking temperature settings between 180° F to 400° F as per your recipe needs. The air fryer having non-stick pan, detachable dishwasher safe basket, and heat resistant handle to make your cleaning process easy.

How does the Ultrean Air Fryer Works?

The Ultrean air fryer works on a very simple technique. The food placed in the air fryer will get a deep fried taste and crunchy texture because of a little oil spread over food. The oil heats quickly and fries your food evenly because oil is the best heat conductor cooks your food faster. The air fryer mechanism is designed in such a way that hot air is circulated directly into the cooking chamber. The Ultrean air fryer is capable to produce 400°F hot air and circulates it around your food to get fast and even cooking results.

The all-in-one Ultrean air fryer allows you to air fry, roast, bake and grill your favorite foods. The air fryer generates heat with the help of heating elements which is exactly fixing over the cooking chamber. There is an exhaust fan given backside of the air fryer which helps to provide the airflow to the air fryer to maintain constant temperature into the cooking chamber to cook your food faster and evenly. It air fry healthy food using 80 percent less oil and fats compare with the deep-frying method.

Before First use

1. First, remove all the packaging material and stickers from the inside and outside surface of the Ultrean air fryer.
2. Now place your air fryer overstable and heat resistant surface. Keep at least 5 inches of space between air fryer and wall to work exhaust system properly.

Test run Ultrean air fryer

Before starting the actual cooking process take a taste run of your Ultrean air fryer. The test run will help you to clean your Ultrean air fryer properly for any residues present during the manufacturing process. It also helps you become familiar with your Ultrean air fryer and their cooking process. The following step by step instructions will help to take the test run of your Ultrean air fryer.

1. First, plug the air fryer into a power socket. Then remove the cooking basket and put lemon or lemon peel into the basket.
2. Now fix the cooking basket into the main unit. Set the temperature at 400°F by pressing + or - button then adjust the timer for 10 minutes by pressing + or - buttons.
3. Now press the power button to start the cooking process. When the timer counts down and reaches zero the air fryer gives bip sound. This indicates that the cooking process finished.
4. Pull out the cooking basket and let it allow cooling down at least 5 minutes. And place the empty cooking basket into its original position.
5. Repeat this process to properly clean and make your air fryer odour free.

Structure of the Ultrean Air Fryer

1. Air Fryer Basket

The air fryer basket is used to hold your food while cooking. It is made up of non-stick coated material. It is Detachable device and you can easily remove it from the main unit. The air fryer basket also comes with food separators to cook multiple foods at once. The air fryer basket is dishwasher safe makes your cleaning process easy.

2. Heating Elements

Heating elements are used to generate the heat required to cook your food. The heating elements are generally situated at the top side of the cooking chamber.

3. Convection fan

Convection fan is situated behind the heating elements. It is used to circulate very hot air into the cooking chamber to cook your food. The even distribution of heat helps to cook your food evenly from all the sides.

4. Exhaust System

To maintain and regulate the inside pressure exhaust system is used. Now, most of the exhaust system contains filters which clean out the exhaust air and doesn't fill your kitchen with fried food smell. The exhaust system is situated on the backside near heating elements.

Benefits of Using Ultrean Air fryer

The air fryer is an advanced cooking device comes with various kinds of benefits. Some of the important benefits are given as follows.

- **Use less oil and fats**

This is one of the major benefits of using an air fryer. It cooks your food using 80 per cent less oil and fats compared with the deep-frying method. If you are one of person who love fried food but worried due to extra calorie intake. Then Ultrean air fryer is best option available in the market. If you want to fries a bowl of French fries or spring rolls then you just need to add a tablespoon of oil or fats to make it tender from inside and crispy brown from outside. It is one of the healthy options to you and your family to cook low-calorie food without compromising the taste and texture of the food.

- **Versatile and economic cooking appliances**

The Ultrean air fryer is one of the versatile cooking appliances comes with various cooking operations like air fry French fries, roast chicken, grill meat and bake your favourite cake and cookies. You never need to buy a separate appliance to perform these cooking tasks. It saves you more than 80 percent of oil and fats so it is economical for cooking appliances to save you money over oil and fats.

- **Saves your cooking time**

The Ultrean air fryer cooks your food by circulating hot air around the food with the help of convection fan. It blows 400°F hot air to cook food faster and evenly. The exhaust fan maintains constant heat into the cooking chamber to get faster and even cooking results. If you are one of those people having a tight schedule or doing the full-time job then Ultrean air fryer is best choice available in the market.

- **Safe to use**

The Ultrean air fryer is one of the safe appliances for daily cooking. It comes with a cooking basket you just need to put your food into the basket and fix the basket with the main unit. It closes from all the sides while cooking your food so there is no risk of hot oil splatters and accidental burns on your skin.

- **Save nutritional values**

In traditional deep frying method, most of the essential vitamin and nutrients are destroyed and bad fats are added into your food. The Ultrean air fryer cooks your food using very less oil and fats during air frying method the nutritional values of the food does not destroy and harmful compounds are not created in air frying method. So air fried food is healthier than deep-fried food.

- **Easy to use**

While cooking your food with Ultrean air fryer you never need to fuss or stir your food like a stovetop. The Ultrean air fryer is easy to operate and use. You just need to place your food into air fryer basket and fix the basket with the main unit. Then select the appropriate cooking function and set time temperature settings as per your recipe needs. During the cooking process shake the air fryer basket a few times to get even cooking results.

- **Easy to clean**

The Ultrean air fryer comes with non-stick detachable and dishwasher safe air fryer basket. You can easily clean these into the dishwasher. When you finish your cooking process there is less grease into the air fryer basket to clean up because the inner surface of the air fryer basket is made up from non-stick material. You can also clean it by using a soft damp cloth.

Cleaning and Maintenance

Cleaning is one of the essential processes done after each use of the appliances. Regular cleaning will help to keep your appliance clean and odour free. It also improves the lifespan of the appliance. Just follow the step by step cleaning instructions given below.

1. First, turn off the appliances and unplug it from the main power socket. Let it cool down before starting the cleaning process. Remove the air fryer basket for fast cooling.
2. Pull out the rack and air fryer basket for cleaning. Both are dishwasher safe you can wash it into the dishwasher or with the help of soapy water. Soak it if needed.
3. Clean the inner portion of the main unit with the help of soft and moist cloth carefully. If you find any food debris overheating elements then clean the heating elements carefully.
4. Wipe-out exterior body of the air fryer with the help of a soft and moist cloth.
5. After drying all the equipment toughly. Place it to their original position. Now your air fryer is ready for next use.

Chapter 2: Breakfast

Savory & Crispy Hash Browns

Preparation Time 10 minutes
Cooking Time 15 minutes
Serve 4

Ingredients:

- 2 eggs
- 1 tbsp everything bagel seasoning
- 1/4 tsp garlic powder
- 1/2 cup almond flour
- 1/2 onion, chopped
- 2 medium potatoes, shredded & squeezed
- Pepper
- Salt

Directions:

1. Add all ingredients into the bowl and mix until well combined.
2. Spray air fryer basket with cooking spray.
3. Make small patties from mixture and place in air fryer basket and cook at 400 F for 5-6 minutes per side or until cooked.
4. Serve and enjoy.

Nutritional Value (Amount per Serving):

- Calories 138
- Fat 4.1 g
- Carbohydrates 20.5 g
- Sugar 2.3 g
- Protein 5.7 g
- Cholesterol 82 mg

Sweet Potato with Cranberries

Preparation Time 10 minutes
Cooking Time 20 minutes
Serve 2

Ingredients:

- 1 large, sweet potato, cut into 1-inch cubes
- 1/4 cup onion, chopped
- 1/2 cup cranberries
- 1/2 tsp chili powder
- 1/2 tsp cinnamon
- 1 tsp olive oil
- 1/4 tsp salt

Directions:

1. Preheat the oven to 400 F.
2. Add sweet potato and remaining ingredients into the bowl and toss well.
3. Add sweet potato mixture into the air fryer basket and cook for 20 minutes. Shake basket twice.
4. Serve and enjoy.

Nutritional Value (Amount per Serving):

- Calories 126
- Fat 2.6 g
- Carbohydrates 23.3 g
- Sugar 7.5 g
- Protein 2.1 g
- Cholesterol 0 mg

Cheese Omelet

Preparation Time 10 minutes
Cooking Time 20 minutes
Serve 6

Ingredients:

- 8 eggs
- 1/4 tsp onion powder
- 1/2 cup milk
- 1/2 cup half and half
- 1/4 tsp garlic powder
- 1/4 cup cheddar cheese, shredded
- Pepper
- Salt

Directions:

1. Preheat the air fryer to 325 F.
2. Spray a baking dish with cooking spray and set it aside.
3. In a bowl, whisk eggs with milk, onion powder, half and half, garlic powder, pepper, and salt.
4. Add cheddar cheese and stir well.
5. Pour egg mixture into the baking dish.
6. Place dish in air fryer basket and cook for 20 minutes.
7. Serve and enjoy.

Nutritional Value (Amount per Serving):

- Calories 140
- Fat 10.1 g
- Carbohydrates 2.6 g
- Sugar 1.5 g
- Protein 9.9 g
- Cholesterol 232 mg

Zucchini Egg Muffins

Preparation Time 10 minutes
Cooking Time 12 minutes
Serve 6

Ingredients:

- 2 eggs
- 1/2 cup mozzarella cheese, shredded
- 1 cup zucchini, shredded & squeezed
- 1/4 tsp garlic powder
- 1/4 cup cornmeal
- 1 tbsp parmesan cheese, grated
- Pepper
- Salt

Directions:

1. Preheat the air fryer to 350 F.
2. In a bowl, whisk eggs with garlic powder, pepper, and salt.
3. Add zucchini, parmesan cheese, mozzarella cheese, and cornmeal and mix well.
4. Pour egg mixture into a silicone muffin molds.
5. Place muffin molds in an air fryer basket and cook for 10-12 minutes.
6. Serve and enjoy.

Nutritional Value (Amount per Serving):

- Calories 65
- Fat 3.1 g
- Carbohydrates 5 g
- Sugar 0.5 g
- Protein 4.7 g
- Cholesterol 59 mg

Greek Egg Muffins

Preparation Time 10 minutes
Cooking Time 15 minutes
Serve 12

Ingredients:

- 4 eggs
- 1/2 cup egg whites
- 1 tsp garlic powder
- 1/4 cup milk
- 1 bell pepper, chopped
- 5 fresh basil leaves, chopped
- 2 tbsp feta cheese, crumbled
- Pepper
- Salt

Directions:

1. Preheat the air fryer to 325 F.
2. In a bowl, whisk eggs, egg whites, garlic powder, milk, pepper, and salt.
3. Add cheese, bell pepper, and basil, and stir well.
4. Pour egg mixture into 12 silicone muffin molds.
5. Place muffin molds in an air fryer basket and cook for 15 minutes.
6. Serve and enjoy.

Nutritional Value (Amount per Serving):

- Calories 37
- Fat 1.9 g
- Carbohydrates 1.4 g
- Sugar 1 g
- Protein 3.5 g
- Cholesterol 56 mg

Crispy Breakfast Potatoes

Preparation Time 10 minutes
Cooking Time 10 minutes
Serve 2

Ingredients:

- 4 potatoes, peeled and cut into 1-inch cubes
- 1/4 tsp chili powder
- 1 tbsp olive oil
- 1/2 tsp garlic powder
- 1/2 tsp smoked paprika
- Pepper
- Salt

Directions:

1. Preheat the air fryer to 375 F.
2. Add potatoes and remaining ingredients into the bowl and toss well.
3. Add potatoes into the air fryer basket and cook for 10 minutes.
4. Serve and enjoy.

Nutritional Value (Amount per Serving):

- Calories 359
- Fat 7.6 g
- Carbohydrates 67.9 g
- Sugar 5.1 g
- Protein 7.4 g
- Cholesterol 0 mg

Herb Egg Breakfast Muffins

Preparation Time 10 minutes
Cooking Time 15 minutes
Serve 6

Ingredients:

- 6 eggs
- 1/2 tbsp fresh dill, chopped
- 1 tbsp fresh parsley, chopped
- 1/2 tbsp fresh basil, chopped
- 1/4 tsp Italian seasoning
- 1/4 cup mozzarella cheese, grated
- Pepper
- Salt

Directions:

1. Preheat the air fryer to 325 F.
2. In a bowl, whisk eggs with pepper and salt. Add remaining ingredients and stir well.
3. Pour egg mixture into the 6 silicone muffin molds.
4. Place muffin molds in an air fryer basket and cook for 15 minutes.
5. Serve and enjoy.

Nutritional Value (Amount per Serving):

- Calories 68
- Fat 4.7 g
- Carbohydrates 0.6 g
- Sugar 0.4 g
- Protein 6 g
- Cholesterol 164 mg

Cheese Egg Bake

Preparation Time 10 minutes
Cooking Time 20 minutes
Serve 3

Ingredients:

- 6 eggs
- 1/4 lb cheddar cheese, grated
- 1/2 cup milk
- 1/4 tsp garlic powder
- Pepper
- Salt

Directions:

1. Preheat the air fryer to 325 F.
2. Spray a baking dish with cooking spray and set it aside.
3. In a bowl, whisk eggs with milk, garlic powder, pepper, and salt. Stir in cheese.
4. Pour egg mixture into the baking dish.
5. Place baking dish in air fryer basket and cook for 20 minutes.
6. Serve and enjoy.

Nutritional Value (Amount per Serving):

- Calories 299
- Fat 22.1 g
- Carbohydrates 3.4 g
- Sugar 2.8 g
- Protein 21.9 g
- Cholesterol 370 mg

Italian Egg Muffins

Preparation Time 10 minutes
Cooking Time 10 minutes
Serve 6

Ingredients:

- 2 eggs
- 1/2 cup milk
- 4 egg whites
- 1/4 cup feta cheese, crumbled
- 1/4 cup olives, diced
- 1/4 cup onion, diced
- 1/4 cup tomatoes, diced
- Pepper
- Salt

Directions:

1. Preheat the air fryer to 325 F.
2. In a bowl, whisk eggs with milk, pepper, and salt. Add remaining ingredients and stir well.
3. Pour egg mixture into the 6 silicone muffin molds.
4. Place muffin molds in an air fryer basket and cook for 10 minutes.
5. Serve and enjoy.

Nutritional Value (Amount per Serving):

- Calories 69
- Fat 3.9 g
- Carbohydrates 2.6 g
- Sugar 1.9 g
- Protein 6 g
- Cholesterol 62 mg

Kale Egg Muffins

Preparation Time 10 minutes
Cooking Time 10 minutes
Serve 6

Ingredients:

- 5 eggs
- 1/4 tsp garlic powder
- 1/4 tsp onion powder
- 1/2 cup mushrooms, chopped
- 1 cup kale, chopped
- Pepper
- Salt

Directions:

1. Preheat the air fryer to 375 F.
2. In a bowl, whisk eggs with garlic powder, onion powder, pepper, and salt.
3. Add kale and mushrooms and stir well.
4. Pour egg mixture into the 6 silicone muffin molds.
5. Place muffin molds in an air fryer basket and cook for 10 minutes.
6. Serve and enjoy.

Nutritional Value (Amount per Serving):

- Calories 60
- Fat 3.7 g
- Carbohydrates 1.8 g
- Sugar 0.5 g
- Protein 5.2 g
- Cholesterol 136 mg

Chapter 3: Poultry Recipes

Juicy Turkey Breast

Preparation Time 10 minutes
Cooking Time 55 minutes
Serve 4

Ingredients:

- 3 lbs turkey breast
- 1/2 tbsp rosemary
- 1/2 tbsp sage
- 1/2 tbsp thyme
- 1 tsp garlic, minced
- 3 tbsp butter, softened
- Pepper
- Salt

Directions:

1. Preheat the oven to 350 F.
2. Spray air fryer basket with cooking spray.
3. In a small bowl, mix butter, garlic, thyme, sage, rosemary, pepper, and salt.
4. Rub turkey breast with butter mixture and place in air fryer basket and cook for 20 minutes.
5. Flip turkey breast and cook for 35 minutes more or until internal temperature reaches 165 F.
6. Slice and serve.

Nutritional Value (Amount per Serving):

- Calories 434
- Fat 14.4 g
- Carbohydrates 15.2 g
- Sugar 12 g
- Protein 58.3 g
- Cholesterol 169 mg

Crispy Chicken Wings

Preparation Time 10 minutes
Cooking Time 30 minutes
Serve 2

Ingredients:

- 1/2 lb chicken wings
- 1/2 packet ranch seasoning
- 2 tsp hot sauce
- 1/4 cup BBQ sauce
- 1/4 cup butter, melted
- Pepper
- Salt

Directions:

1. Season chicken wings with pepper and salt.
2. Add chicken wings into the air fryer basket and cook at 360 F for 12 minutes.
3. Flip chicken wings and cook for 12 minutes.
4. Turn temperature to 390 F and cook chicken wings for 6 minutes more.
5. In a large bowl, add butter, ranch seasoning, hot sauce, and BBQ sauce and mix well.
6. Add chicken wings to the large bowl and toss well.
7. Serve and enjoy.

Nutritional Value (Amount per Serving):

- Calories 488
- Fat 31.5 g
- Carbohydrates 11.5 g
- Sugar 8.2 g
- Protein 33.1 g
- Cholesterol 162 mg

Flavorful Lemon Pepper Wings

Preparation Time 10 minutes
Cooking Time 25 minutes
Serve 4

Ingredients:

- 1 1/2 lbs chicken wings
- 1/4 tsp cayenne
- 2 tsp lemon pepper seasoning
- 1 tsp honey
- 3 tbsp butter, melted

Directions:

1. Preheat the air fryer to 380 F.
2. Season chicken wings with cayenne and lemon pepper seasoning.
3. Place chicken wings into the air fryer basket and cook for 20 minutes. Flip wings halfway through.
4. Turn temperature to 400 F and cook for 5 minutes more.
5. In a small bowl, mix honey and butter.
6. Transfer chicken wings to the bowl. Pour honey-butter mixture over chicken wings and toss well.
7. Serve and enjoy.

Nutritional Value (Amount per Serving):

- Calories 408
- Fat 21.3 g
- Carbohydrates 2.2 g
- Sugar 1.5 g
- Protein 49.4 g
- Cholesterol 174 mg

Meatballs

Preparation Time 10 minutes
Cooking Time 9 minutes
Serve 4

Ingredients:

- 1 egg
- 1 lb ground chicken
- 1 tsp onion powder
- 1 tsp lemon zest
- 1 tbsp dried oregano
- 1 1/2 tbsp ginger garlic paste
- Pepper
- Salt

Directions:

1. Preheat the air fryer to 390 F.
2. Spray air fryer basket with cooking spray.
3. Add all ingredients into the bowl and mix until well combined.
4. Make small balls from the meat mixture and place them into the air fryer basket and cook for 8-9 minutes or until internal temperature reaches 160 F.
5. Serve and enjoy.

Nutritional Value (Amount per Serving):

- Calories 247
- Fat 10 g
- Carbohydrates 2.5 g
- Sugar 0.4 g
- Protein 34.8 g
- Cholesterol 142 mg

Flavorful Chicken Fajitas

Preparation Time 10 minutes
Cooking Time 10 minutes
Serve 4

Ingredients:

- 1/2 lb chicken breasts, boneless & cut into strips
- 1 tsp cumin
- 2 tsp lime juice
- 1 tbsp chili powder
- 1 tbsp olive oil
- 1 onion, sliced
- 1 bell pepper, sliced
- 1/8 tsp cayenne
- Pepper
- Salt

Directions:

1. Preheat the air fryer to 370 F.
2. Add chicken and remaining ingredients into the bowl and toss well.
3. Add chicken mixture into the air fryer basket and cook for 10 minutes or until internal temperature reaches 165 F.
4. Serve and enjoy.

Nutritional Value (Amount per Serving):

- Calories 172
- Fat 8.3 g
- Carbohydrates 8 g
- Sugar 3.2 g
- Protein 17.4 g
- Cholesterol 50 mg

Easy BBQ Chicken

Preparation Time: 10 minutes
Cooking Time: 14 minutes
Serve: 2

Ingredients:

- 2 chicken breasts, boneless & skinless
- 1 tbsp BBQ seasoning

Directions:

1. Preheat the air fryer to 400 F.
2. Rub chicken breasts with BBQ seasoning and place in the refrigerator for 30 minutes.
3. Place chicken into the air fryer basket and cook for 14 minutes. Flip chicken halfway through.
4. Serve and enjoy.

Nutritional Value (Amount per Serving):

- Calories 283
- Fat 10.9 g
- Carbohydrates 0.7 g
- Sugar 0.2 g
- Protein 42.6 g
- Cholesterol 130 mg

Juicy Turkey Patties

Preparation Time: 10 minutes
Cooking Time: 14 minutes
Serve: 2

Ingredients:

- 1/2 ground turkey
- 2 tbsp breadcrumbs
- 1 tsp Worcestershire sauce
- 1/2 tbsp ranch seasoning
- 1/4 onion, grated
- 2 tbsp apple sauce
- Pepper
- Salt

Directions:

1. Preheat the air fryer to 360 F.
2. Add all ingredients into the bowl and mix until well combined.
3. Make two patties from the mixture and place them into the air fryer basket and cook for 14 minutes. Turn patties halfway through.
4. Serve and enjoy.

Nutritional Value (Amount per Serving):

- Calories 206
- Fat 9.4 g
- Carbohydrates 7.4 g
- Sugar 2.2 g
- Protein 23.6 g
- Cholesterol 84 mg

Quick Chicken Patties

Preparation Time: 10 minutes
Cooking Time: 12 minutes
Serve: 6

Ingredients:

- 1 lb ground chicken
- 1/2 tsp Italian seasoning
- 1/2 tsp garlic powder
- 1 tsp onion powder
- 1/2 cup parmesan cheese, grated
- 1/4 cup Greek yogurt
- Pepper
- Salt

Directions:

1. Preheat the air fryer to 400 F.
2. Add all ingredients into the bowl and mix until well combined.
3. Make patties from the mixture and place them into the air fryer basket and cook for 12 minutes. Flip patties halfway through.
4. Serve and enjoy.

Nutritional Value (Amount per Serving):

- Calories 177
- Fat 7.5 g
- Carbohydrates 1.2 g
- Sugar 0.6 g
- Protein 25.2 g
- Cholesterol 73 mg

Cajun Chicken Nuggets

Preparation Time: 10 minutes
Cooking Time: 12 minutes
Serve: 4

Ingredients:

- 1 lb chicken breast, boneless, skinless & diced
- 1 tbsp olive oil
- 1/2 tsp red chili flakes
- 1/2 tsp dried oregano
- 1/2 tsp onion powder
- 1/2 tsp garlic powder
- 1 tsp smoked paprika
- 1/2 tbsp sugar
- Pepper
- Salt

Directions:

1. Preheat the air fryer to 400 F.
2. Add all ingredients into the bowl and mix until well coated.
3. Add chicken into the air fryer basket and cook for 12 minutes.
4. Serve and enjoy.

Nutritional Value (Amount per Serving):

- Calories 169
- Fat 6.4 g
- Carbohydrates 2.4 g
- Sugar 1.8 g
- Protein 24.2 g
- Cholesterol 73 mg

Healthy Greek Chicken

Preparation Time: 10 minutes
Cooking Time: 12 minutes
Serve: 2

Ingredients:

- 10 oz chicken breast, boneless & cut into cubes
- 2 tbsp feta cheese, crumbled
- 1 1/2 tbsp olive oil
- 1/4 tsp dried thyme
- 1/2 tsp garlic powder
- 1/2 tsp dried parsley
- 1 tsp dried oregano
- 1/2 zucchini, chopped
- 1/2 bell pepper, chopped
- 1/2 onion, chopped
- Pepper
- Salt

Directions:

1. Preheat the air fryer to 380 F.
2. Add chicken and remaining ingredients except for feta cheese into the mixing bowl and mix well.
3. Add chicken mixture into the air fryer basket and cook for 12 minutes.
4. Top with crumbled cheese and serve.

Nutritional Value (Amount per Serving):

- Calories 310
- Fat 16.3 g
- Carbohydrates 8 g
- Sugar 4.1 g
- Protein 32.8 g
- Cholesterol 99 mg

Sesame Chicken

Preparation Time: 10 minutes
Cooking Time: 30 minutes
Serve: 2

Ingredients:

- 2 chicken breasts, boneless
- 1 tsp onion powder
- 1 tsp garlic powder
- 1/4 tsp cayenne pepper
- 1 tbsp sweet paprika
- 1/2 tsp pepper
- 2 tbsp sesame oil
- 1 tsp kosher salt

Directions:

1. Preheat the air fryer to 380 F.
2. In a small bowl, mix onion powder, garlic powder, cayenne, sweet paprika, pepper, and salt.
3. Brush chicken breasts with sesame oil and rub with spice mixture.
4. Place chicken breasts into the air fryer basket and cook for 30 minutes. Turn chicken after 20 minutes.
5. Serve and enjoy.

Nutritional Value (Amount per Serving):

- Calories 418
- Fat 25 g
- Carbohydrates 4.4 g
- Sugar 1.2 g
- Protein 43.2 g
- Cholesterol 130 mg

Buffalo Meatballs

Preparation Time: 10 minutes
Cooking Time: 12 minutes
Serve: 4

Ingredients:

- 1 egg
- 1 lb ground chicken
- 1/2 tsp onion powder
- 1/2 tsp garlic powder
- 1/4 cup buffalo sauce
- 1/2 cup breadcrumbs
- Pepper
- Salt

Directions:

1. Preheat the air fryer to 400 F.
2. Add all ingredients into the bowl and mix until well combined.
3. Make meatballs from the mixture and place them into the air fryer basket and cook for 12 minutes.
4. Serve and enjoy.

Nutritional Value (Amount per Serving):

- Calories 288
- Fat 10.2 g
- Carbohydrates 10.4 g
- Sugar 1.1 g
- Protein 36.1 g
- Cholesterol 142 mg

Jerk Chicken Wings

Preparation Time: 10 minutes
Cooking Time: 25 minutes
Serve: 2

Ingredients:

- 1 lb chicken wings
- 1 tbsp Jerk seasoning
- 1 tbsp olive oil

Directions:

1. Preheat the air fryer to 400 F.
2. Brush chicken wings with oil and rub with jerk seasoning.
3. Place chicken wings into the air fryer basket and cook for 20-25 minutes. Turn chicken wings halfway through.
4. Serve and enjoy.

Nutritional Value (Amount per Serving):

- Calories 491
- Fat 23.8 g
- Carbohydrates 0 g
- Sugar 0 g
- Protein 65.6 g
- Cholesterol 202 mg

Crispy Chicken Drumsticks

Preparation Time: 10 minutes
Cooking Time: 20 minutes
Serve: 4

Ingredients:

- 6 chicken drumsticks
- 1/2 tsp garlic powder
- 1/2 tsp smoked paprika
- 2 tbsp olive oil
- 1/4 tsp pepper
- 1/2 tsp salt

Directions:

1. Preheat the air fryer to 390 F.
2. Brush chicken drumsticks with oil and season with garlic powder, paprika, pepper, and salt.
3. Place chicken drumsticks into the air fryer basket and cook for 20 minutes. Turn chicken drumsticks halfway through.
4. Serve and enjoy.

Nutritional Value (Amount per Serving):

- Calories 179
- Fat 11 g
- Carbohydrates 0.5 g
- Sugar 0.1 g
- Protein 19.1 g
- Cholesterol 61 mg

Tender & Flavorful Chicken Breast

Preparation Time: 10 minutes
Cooking Time: 20 minutes
Serve: 4

Ingredients:

- 2 chicken breasts, skinless
- 1 tsp onion powder
- 1/2 tsp dried rosemary
- 1 tsp oregano
- 1 tsp ground thyme
- 1/2 tsp pepper
- 1/2 tsp salt

Directions:

1. Preheat the air fryer to 350 F.
2. Mix onion powder, rosemary, oregano, thyme, pepper, and salt and rub over chicken breasts.
3. Place chicken breasts into the air fryer basket and cook for 20 minutes. Turn chicken halfway through.
4. Serve and enjoy.

Nutritional Value (Amount per Serving):

- Calories 144
- Fat 5.5 g
- Carbohydrates 1.2 g
- Sugar 0.2 g
- Protein 21.3 g
- Cholesterol 65 mg

Juicy & Tasty Chicken Tenders

Preparation Time: 10 minutes
Cooking Time: 13 minutes
Serve: 4

Ingredients:

- 6 chicken tenders
- 1 tsp onion powder
- 1 tsp oregano
- 1 tsp garlic powder
- 1 tsp paprika
- 1 tsp kosher salt

Directions:

1. Preheat the air fryer to 380 F.
2. Add chicken tenders and remaining ingredients into the zip-lock bag, seal bag and shake well to coat.
3. Place chicken tenders into the air fryer basket and cook for 13 minutes.
4. Serve and enjoy.

Nutritional Value (Amount per Serving):

- Calories 423
- Fat 16.4 g
- Carbohydrates 1.5 g
- Sugar 0.5 g
- Protein 63.7 g
- Cholesterol 195 mg

Easy Turkey Burger Patties

Preparation Time: 10 minutes
Cooking Time: 12 minutes
Serve: 4

Ingredients:

- 1 lb ground turkey
- 1 tsp garlic, minced
- 1 shallot, diced
- 1 jalapeno, diced
- Pepper
- Salt

Directions:

1. Preheat the air fryer to 380 F.
2. Add all ingredients into the bowl and mix until well combined.
3. Make four patties from the mixture and place them into the air fryer basket and cook for 12 minutes or until cooked.
4. Serve and enjoy.

Nutritional Value (Amount per Serving):

- Calories 225
- Fat 12.5 g
- Carbohydrates 0.9 g
- Sugar 0.1 g
- Protein 31.2 g
- Cholesterol 116 mg

Turkey Meatballs

Preparation Time: 10 minutes
Cooking Time: 10 minutes
Serve: 4

Ingredients:

- 1 egg
- 1 lb ground turkey
- 1 tsp soy sauce
- 1/4 cup parsley, chopped
- 1/2 cup breadcrumbs
- Pepper
- Salt

Directions:

1. Preheat the air fryer to 400 F.
2. Add all ingredients into the bowl and mix until well combined.
3. Make small balls from the mixture and place them into the air fryer basket and cook for 10 minutes. Turn halfway through.
4. Serve and enjoy.

Nutritional Value (Amount per Serving):

- Calories 292
- Fat 14.3 g
- Carbohydrates 10.2 g
- Sugar 1 g
- Protein 34.4 g
- Cholesterol 157 mg

Meatballs

Preparation Time: 10 minutes
Cooking Time: 15 minutes
Serve: 4

Ingredients:

- 1 lb ground chicken
- 1/4 cup shredded coconut
- 1 tsp olive oil
- 1 tsp hot sauce
- 1 tbsp soy sauce
- 1 tbsp Hoisin sauce
- 1/2 cup parsley, chopped
- 2 green scallions, chopped
- Pepper
- Salt

Directions:

1. Preheat the air fryer to 350 F.
2. Add all ingredients into the bowl and mix until well combined.
3. Make small balls from the mixture and place them into the air fryer basket and cook for 15 minutes.
4. Serve and enjoy.

Nutritional Value (Amount per Serving):

- Calories 262
- Fat 11.4 g
- Carbohydrates 4.3 g
- Sugar 2.1 g
- Protein 33.6 g
- Cholesterol 101 mg

Asian Chicken Patties

Preparation Time: 10 minutes
Cooking Time: 12 minutes
Serve: 2

Ingredients:

- 8 oz ground chicken
- 1/4 tsp onion powder
- 1/4 tsp garlic powder
- 2 tbsp sweet chili sauce
- 1/4 cup scallions, chopped
- 1/4 cup can water chestnuts, drained & chopped
- Pepper
- Salt

Directions:

1. Preheat the air fryer to 390 F.
2. Add all ingredients into the bowl and mix until well combined.
3. Make patties from the mixture and place them into the air fryer basket and cook for 12 minutes.
4. Serve and enjoy.

Nutritional Value (Amount per Serving):

- Calories 255
- Fat 8.5 g
- Carbohydrates 7.9 g
- Sugar 6.8 g
- Protein 33.4 g
- Cholesterol 101 mg

Cajun Chicken Thighs

Preparation Time: 10 minutes
Cooking Time: 15 minutes
Serve: 4

Ingredients:

- 4 chicken thighs, boneless
- 1/2 tsp Cajun seasoning
- 1 tsp paprika
- 1/3 cup breadcrumbs
- 1 tbsp olive oil
- 4 tbsp parmesan cheese, grated
- Pepper
- Salt

Directions:

1. Preheat the air fryer to 400 F.
2. In a bowl, mix breadcrumbs, parmesan cheese, paprika, Cajun seasoning, pepper, and salt.
3. Brush chicken thighs with oil and coat with breadcrumb mixture.
4. Place coated chicken in an air fryer basket and cook for 15 minutes.
5. Serve and enjoy.

Nutritional Value (Amount per Serving):

- Calories 435
- Fat 20.9 g
- Carbohydrates 7.8 g
- Sugar 0.6 g
- Protein 52.5 g
- Cholesterol 150 mg

Greek Meatballs

Preparation Time: 10 minutes
Cooking Time: 10 minutes
Serve: 4

Ingredients:

- 1 lb ground chicken
- 1/4 cup sun-dried tomatoes, drained
- 3 cups spinach, chopped
- 3/4 cup breadcrumbs
- 1/4 cup goat cheese, crumbled
- 2 tbsp parmesan cheese, grated
- Pepper
- Salt

Directions:

1. Preheat the air fryer to 400 F.
2. Add spinach and tomatoes into the food processor and process until smooth. Add spinach mixture into the bowl.
3. Add remaining ingredients into the bowl and mix until well combined.
4. Make balls from the meat mixture and place them in the air fryer basket and cook for 10 minutes.
5. Serve and enjoy.

Nutritional Value (Amount per Serving):

- Calories 356
- Fat 13.2 g
- Carbohydrates 16.4 g
- Sugar 1.7 g
- Protein 41.3 g
- Cholesterol 113 mg

Simple Adobo Chicken

Preparation Time: 10 minutes
Cooking Time: 20 minutes
Serve: 4

Ingredients:

- 4 chicken thighs
- 1 1/2 tbsp Adobo seasoning
- 1 tbsp butter, melted
- Pepper
- Salt

Directions:

1. Preheat the air fryer to 350 F.
2. In a small bowl, mix butter, Adobo seasoning, pepper, and salt and brush over chicken.
3. Place chicken thighs in an air fryer basket and cook for 20 minutes.
4. Serve and enjoy.

Nutritional Value (Amount per Serving):

- Calories 303
- Fat 13.7 g
- Carbohydrates 0 g
- Sugar 0 g
- Protein 42.3 g
- Cholesterol 138 mg

Mustard Chicken Tenders

Preparation Time: 10 minutes
Cooking Time: 20 minutes
Serve: 4

Ingredients:

- 1 lb chicken tenders
- 1 tsp garlic, minced
- 1/2 tsp smoked paprika
- 2 tbsp fresh tarragon, chopped
- 1/2 oz fresh lemon juice
- 1/2 cup whole grain mustard
- 1/4 tsp kosher salt

Directions:

1. Preheat the air fryer to 380 F.
2. Add all ingredients except chicken to the bowl and mix well.
3. Add chicken and mix until well coated.
4. Place chicken tenders in an air fryer basket and cook for 20 minutes. Turn chicken halfway through.
5. Serve and enjoy.

Nutritional Value (Amount per Serving):

- Calories 241
- Fat 9.5 g
- Carbohydrates 2.9 g
- Sugar 0.1 g
- Protein 33.1 g
- Cholesterol 101 mg

Crispy Chicken Breast

Preparation Time: 10 minutes
Cooking Time: 14 minutes
Serve: 2

Ingredients:

- 2 chicken breasts, boneless
- 2 cups crushed crackers
- 1 tbsp butter, melted
- Pepper
- Salt

Directions:

1. Preheat the air fryer to 370 F.
2. Season chicken with pepper, and salt.
3. Brush chicken with butter and coat with crushed crackers.
4. Place chicken in air fryer basket and cook for 14 minutes.
5. Serve and enjoy.

Nutritional Value (Amount per Serving):

- Calories 448
- Fat 22.6 g
- Carbohydrates 15 g
- Sugar 3 g
- Protein 44.3 g
- Cholesterol 145 mg

Chapter 4: Beef, Pork & Lamb

Simple & Juicy Pork Chops

Preparation Time 10 minutes
Cooking Time 10 minutes
Serve 4

Ingredients:

- 4 pork chops, boneless
- 1 tsp Italian seasoning
- 1 tsp olive oil
- Pepper
- Salt

Directions:

1. Preheat the air fryer to 400 F.
2. In a small bowl, mix oil, Italian seasoning, pepper, and salt.
3. Brush pork chops with oil mixture and place in an air fryer basket.
4. Cook pork chops for 10 minutes or until the internal temperature reaches 145 F.
5. Serve and enjoy.

Nutritional Value (Amount per Serving):

- Calories 270
- Fat 21.4 g
- Carbohydrates 0.2 g
- Sugar 0.1 g
- Protein 18 g
- Cholesterol 70 mg

Sweet & Spicy Pork Chops

Preparation Time 10 minutes
Cooking Time 14 minutes
Serve 4

Ingredients:

- 4 pork chops
- 1 tbsp olive oil
- 1 tbsp sweet chili sauce
- 2 tbsp fresh lemon juice
- 1 tbsp garlic, minced
- 1/4 cup honey
- Pepper
- Salt

Directions:

1. Preheat the air fryer to 400 F.
2. Season pork chops with pepper and salt and place in an air fryer basket.
3. Cook pork chops for 10 minutes or until the internal temperature reaches 145 F.
4. Meanwhile, heat oil in a pan over medium heat.
5. Add garlic and saute for 30 seconds. Add chili sauce, lemon juice, and honey, and cook until sauce thickens about 3-4 minutes.
6. Place pork chops on a plate.
7. Pour sauce over pork chops and serve.

Nutritional Value (Amount per Serving):

- Calories 363
- Fat 23.5 g
- Carbohydrates 19.8 g
- Sugar 19.1 g
- Protein 18.2 g
- Cholesterol 69 mg

Mexican Meatballs

Preparation Time 10 minutes
Cooking Time 10 minutes
Serve 4

Ingredients:

- 1 egg
- 1 lb ground beef
- 1/2 cup cheddar cheese, shredded
- 2 tbsp taco seasoning
- 1/4 cup onions, chopped
- Pepper
- Salt

Directions:

1. Preheat the air fryer to 400 F.
2. Spray air fryer basket with cooking spray.
3. Add all ingredients into the bowl and mix until well combined.
4. Make small balls from the mixture and place them into the air fryer basket and cook for 10 minutes.
5. Serve and enjoy.

Nutritional Value (Amount per Serving):

- Calories 296
- Fat 13.4 g
- Carbohydrates 1.7 g
- Sugar 0.5 g
- Protein 39.9 g
- Cholesterol 159 mg

Meatballs

Preparation Time: 10 minutes
Cooking Time: 10 minutes
Serve: 8

Ingredients:

- 2 eggs, lightly beaten
- 1 tbsp Worcestershire sauce
- 1/2 cup feta cheese, crumbled
- 1/2 cup breadcrumbs
- 1/4 cup fresh parsley, chopped
- 1 tbsp garlic, minced
- 1 onion, chopped
- 1 lb ground pork
- 1 lb ground beef
- Pepper
- Salt

Directions:

1. Preheat the air fryer to 400 F.
2. Add all ingredients into the food processor and process until well combined.
3. Make small balls from the meat mixture and place them into the air fryer basket and cook for 10 minutes.
4. Serve and enjoy.

Nutritional Value (Amount per Serving):

- Calories 263
- Fat 9 g
- Carbohydrates 7.5 g
- Sugar 1.9 g
- Protein 35.9 g
- Cholesterol 141 mg

Juicy Pork Chops

Preparation Time: 10 minutes
Cooking Time: 14 minutes
Serve: 2

Ingredients:

- 2 pork chops
- 1/2 tsp garlic powder
- 1/2 tsp paprika
- 1/2 tsp rosemary
- 1 tsp oregano
- 1 tsp thyme
- 1 tsp sage
- 1 tbsp olive oil
- Pepper
- Salt

Directions:

1. Preheat the air fryer to 360 F.
2. Brush pork chops with oil.
3. In a small bowl, mix garlic powder, paprika, rosemary, oregano, thyme, sage, pepper, and salt and rub over pork chops.
4. Place pork chops into the air fryer basket and cook for 14 minutes. Turn pork chops halfway through.
5. Serve and enjoy.

Nutritional Value (Amount per Serving):

- Calories 326
- Fat 27.2 g
- Carbohydrates 2 g
- Sugar 0.3 g
- Protein 18.4 g
- Cholesterol 69 mg

Meatballs

Preparation Time: 10 minutes
Cooking Time: 10 minutes
Serve: 6

Ingredients:

- 1 egg
- 1/3 cup breadcrumbs
- 1 tbsp garlic, minced
- 1/3 cup parmesan cheese, grated
- 2 tbsp onion soup mix
- 1/2 onion, diced
- 1 1/2 lbs ground beef
- Pepper
- Salt

Directions:

1. Preheat the air fryer to 350 F.
2. Add all ingredients into the bowl and mix until well combined.
3. Make balls from the mixture and place them into the air fryer basket and cook for 10 minutes. Turn meatballs halfway through.
4. Serve and enjoy.

Nutritional Value (Amount per Serving):

- Calories 263
- Fat 8.5 g
- Carbohydrates 7.3 g
- Sugar 0.9 g
- Protein 37 g
- Cholesterol 130 mg

Delicious Steak Fajitas

Preparation Time: 10 minutes
Cooking Time: 12 minutes
Serve: 4

Ingredients:

- 1 lb steak, sliced
- 2 1/2 tbsp fajita seasoning
- 1/2 onion, sliced
- 1 bell pepper, sliced
- Pepper
- Salt

Directions:

1. Preheat the air fryer to 375 F.
2. Add all ingredients into the bowl and toss well.
3. Add steak mixture into the air fryer basket and cook for 12 minutes. Stir halfway through.
4. Serve and enjoy.

Nutritional Value (Amount per Serving):

- Calories 260
- Fat 5.8 g
- Carbohydrates 7.5 g
- Sugar 2.1 g
- Protein 41.4 g
- Cholesterol 102 mg

Air Fryer Perfect Steak

Preparation Time: 10 minutes
Cooking Time: 18 minutes
Serve: 2

Ingredients:

- 2 steaks
- 1/2 tsp garlic powder
- 1 tsp olive oil
- 1/4 tsp onion powder
- 1/4 tsp smoked paprika
- Pepper
- Salt

Directions:

1. Preheat the air fryer to 400 F.
2. Brush steak with oil and season with garlic powder, onion powder, paprika, pepper, and salt.
3. Place steaks into the air fryer basket and cook for 18 minutes.
4. Serve and enjoy.

Nutritional Value (Amount per Serving):

- Calories 193
- Fat 6.6 g
- Carbohydrates 0.9 g
- Sugar 0.3 g
- Protein 30.9 g
- Cholesterol 77 mg

Steak Bites

Preparation Time: 10 minutes
Cooking Time: 18 minutes
Serve: 4

Ingredients:

- 1 lb steaks, cut into 1-inch cubes
- 1/2 tsp garlic powder
- 1 tsp Worcestershire sauce
- 2 tbsp butter, melted
- Pepper
- Salt

Directions:

1. Preheat the air fryer to 400 F.
2. Add steak cubes and remaining ingredients into the bowl and toss well.
3. Add steak cubes into the air fryer basket and cook for 18 minutes. Stir halfway through.
4. Serve and enjoy.

Nutritional Value (Amount per Serving):

- Calories 279
- Fat 11.4 g
- Carbohydrates 0.5 g
- Sugar 0.3 g
- Protein 41.1 g
- Cholesterol 117 mg

Sweet & Juicy Pork Chops

Preparation Time: 10 minutes
Cooking Time: 14 minutes
Serve: 2

Ingredients:

- 2 pork chops
- 1 1/2 tbsp olive oil
- 2 tbsp honey
- 1 1/2 tbsp mesquite seasoning
- Pepper
- Salt

Directions:

1. Preheat the air fryer to 380 F.
2. Add pork chops and remaining ingredients into the mixing bowl and coat well. Cover and place in the refrigerator for 30 minutes.
3. Place pork chops into the air fryer basket and cook for 14 minutes. Turn pork chops halfway through.
4. Serve and enjoy.

Nutritional Value (Amount per Serving):

- Calories 420
- Fat 30.6 g
- Carbohydrates 19.1 g
- Sugar 17.3 g
- Protein 18.4 g
- Cholesterol 69 mg

Flavorful Steak Bites

Preparation Time: 10 minutes
Cooking Time: 10 minutes
Serve: 4

Ingredients:

- 16 oz steak, cut into cubes
- 1/4 tsp onion powder
- 1/4 tsp garlic powder
- 1 tsp chili powder
- 1/2 tbsp brown sugar
- 1/2 tbsp olive oil
- Pepper
- Salt

Directions:

1. Preheat the air fryer to 400 F.
2. Add steak cubes and remaining ingredients into the bowl and toss well.
3. Add steak cubes into the air fryer basket and cook for 10 minutes. Stir halfway through.
4. Serve and enjoy.

Nutritional Value (Amount per Serving):

- Calories 248
- Fat 7.5 g
- Carbohydrates 1.7 g
- Sugar 1.2 g
- Protein 41.1 g
- Cholesterol 102 mg

Tender & Juicy Pork Chops

Preparation Time: 10 minutes
Cooking Time: 12 minutes
Serve: 4

Ingredients:

- 4 pork chops, boneless
- 1 tsp onion powder
- 1/2 tsp garlic powder
- 1 tsp olive oil
- 1 tsp smoked paprika
- Pepper
- Salt

Directions:

1. Preheat the air fryer to 380 F.
2. In a small bowl, mix onion powder, paprika, garlic powder, pepper, and salt.
3. Brush pork chops with oil and rub with spice mixture.
4. Place pork chops into the air fryer basket and cook for 12 minutes. Turn pork chops halfway through.
5. Serve and enjoy.

Nutritional Value (Amount per Serving):

- Calories 271
- Fat 21.1 g
- Carbohydrates 1.1 g
- Sugar 0.4 g
- Protein 18.2 g
- Cholesterol 69 mg

Marinated Pork Chops

Preparation Time: 10 minutes
Cooking Time: 12 minutes
Serve: 4

Ingredients:

- 4 pork chops, boneless
- 1 tsp lemon juice
- 1 tsp Worcestershire sauce
- 1 tbsp soy sauce
- 2 tbsp brown sugar
- 1/4 tsp pepper
- 1/4 tsp salt

Directions:

1. Preheat the air fryer to 370 F.
2. Add pork chops and remaining ingredients into the zip-lock bag. Seal bag, shake well and place in the refrigerator for 30 minutes.
3. Place pork chops into the air fryer basket and cook for 12 minutes. Turn pork chops halfway through.
4. Serve and enjoy.

Nutritional Value (Amount per Serving):

- Calories 277
- Fat 19.9 g
- Carbohydrates 5.1 g
- Sugar 4.7 g
- Protein 18.3 g
- Cholesterol 69 mg

Brined Pork Chops

Preparation Time: 10 minutes
Cooking Time: 12 minutes
Serve: 4

Ingredients:

- 4 pork chops, boneless
- 1/2 tsp garlic powder
- 1/2 tsp chili powder
- 2 tbsp brown sugar
- 1 tsp peppercorns
- 2 tbsp sugar
- Salt

Directions:

1. Preheat the air fryer to 400 F.
2. Add 4 cups water, 1/4 cup kosher salt, sugar, and peppercorns into the saucepan and bring to boil.
3. Once sugar dissolved completely then remove the saucepan from heat and let it cool completely.
4. Pour brine over pork chops and let sit for 30 minutes. Drain well and pat dry pork chops with a paper towel.
5. Mix together garlic powder, chili powder, and brown sugar and rub over pork chops.
6. Place pork chops into the air fryer basket and cook for 12 minutes. Turn pork chops halfway through.
7. Serve and enjoy.

Nutritional Value (Amount per Serving):

- Calories 299
- Fat 20 g
- Carbohydrates 11.2 g
- Sugar 10.5 g
- Protein 18.2 g
- Cholesterol 69 mg

Asian Meatballs

Preparation Time: 10 minutes
Cooking Time: 10 minutes
Serve: 4

Ingredients:

- 2 eggs
- 2 lbs ground pork
- 1/3 tsp chili flakes
- 1 tbsp green onion, chopped
- 1 tsp soy sauce
- 1 tsp sesame oil
- 1 1/2 tsp ginger garlic paste
- 1/2 cup breadcrumbs
- Pepper
- Salt

Directions:

1. Preheat the air fryer to 400 F.
2. Add all ingredients into the bowl and mix until well combined.
3. Make small balls from the mixture and place them into the air fryer basket and cook for 10 minutes. Turn meatballs halfway through.
4. Serve and enjoy.

Nutritional Value (Amount per Serving):

- Calories 430
- Fat 12.4 g
- Carbohydrates 11.3 g
- Sugar 1.1 g
- Protein 64.4 g
- Cholesterol 247 mg

Dijon Lamb Chops

Preparation Time: 10 minutes
Cooking Time: 18 minutes
Serve: 2

Ingredients:

- 8 lamb chops
- 1 tsp cayenne
- 1 tsp cumin powder
- 1 tsp garlic, minced
- 1 tsp soy sauce
- 2 tsp olive oil
- 2 tsp Dijon mustard
- 1/4 tsp salt

Directions:

1. Preheat the air fryer to 350 F.
2. Add lamb chops and remaining ingredients into the zip-lock bag. Seal bag, shake well and place in the refrigerator for 30 minutes.
3. Place lamb chops into the air fryer basket and cook for 18 minutes. Turn lamb chops halfway through.
4. Serve and enjoy.

Nutritional Value (Amount per Serving):

- Calories 814
- Fat 45.3 g
- Carbohydrates 1.9 g
- Sugar 0.2 g
- Protein 92.8 g
- Cholesterol 300 mg

Baked Meatballs

Preparation Time: 10 minutes
Cooking Time: 20 minutes
Serve: 4

Ingredients:

- 1 lb ground lamb
- 1/4 tsp dried basil
- 1/4 tsp dried oregano
- 1 garlic clove, minced
- 1/4 cup fresh cilantro, chopped
- 1/4 cup raisins
- 1/4 cup yogurt
- 2 bread slices, cut into small pieces
- 1/8 tsp pepper
- 1/8 tsp salt

Directions:

1. Preheat the air fryer to 375 F.
2. Add all ingredients into the bowl and mix until well combined.
3. Make small balls from the mixture and place them into the air fryer basket and cook for 20 minutes. Turn meatballs halfway through.
4. Serve and enjoy.

Nutritional Value (Amount per Serving):

- Calories 263
- Fat 8.7 g
- Carbohydrates 10.9 g
- Sugar 6.7 g
- Protein 33.4 g
- Cholesterol 103 mg

Meatballs

Preparation Time: 10 minutes
Cooking Time: 20 minutes
Serve: 4

Ingredients:

- 1 egg
- 16 oz ground pork
- 1/4 cup parmesan cheese, grated
- 1/2 onion, diced
- 1/2 tsp pepper
- 1/2 cup breadcrumbs
- 1/4 cup parsley, chopped
- 1 tbsp garlic, minced
- 1/2 tsp kosher salt

Directions:

1. Preheat the air fryer to 400 F.
2. Add all ingredients into the bowl and mix until well combined.
3. Make small balls from the mixture and place them into the air fryer basket and cook for 15-20 minutes. Turn meatballs halfway through.
4. Serve and enjoy.

Nutritional Value (Amount per Serving):

- Calories 247
- Fat 6.2 g
- Carbohydrates 12.2 g
- Sugar 1.6 g
- Protein 33.8 g
- Cholesterol 125 mg

Air Fryer Pork Ribs

Preparation Time: 10 minutes
Cooking Time: 40 minutes
Serve: 4

Ingredients:

- 1 lb baby pork ribs
- 1/2 tbsp Worcestershire sauce
- 1 tbsp hoisin sauce
- 1 tbsp olive oil
- 1 tbsp ginger garlic paste

Directions:

1. Preheat the air fryer to 320 F.
2. In a bowl add all ingredients and coat well. Cover and place in the refrigerator for 1 hour.
3. Place marinated ribs into the air fryer basket and cook for 40 minutes. Turn pork ribs halfway through.
4. Serve and enjoy.

Nutritional Value (Amount per Serving):

- Calories 368
- Fat 31 g
- Carbohydrates 2.9 g
- Sugar 1.5 g
- Protein 18.4 g
- Cholesterol 90 mg

Simple & Delicious Pork Chops

Preparation Time: 10 minutes
Cooking Time: 14 minutes
Serve: 2

Ingredients:

- 2 pork chops, rinsed and pat dry
- 1/2 tsp smoked paprika
- 2 tsp olive oil
- 1/4 tsp pepper
- Salt

Directions:

1. Preheat the air fryer to 380 F.
2. Brush pork chops with oil and season with paprika, pepper, and salt.
3. Place pork chops into the air fryer basket and cook for 14 minutes. Turn pork chops halfway through.
4. Serve and enjoy.

Nutritional Value (Amount per Serving):

- Calories 298
- Fat 24.6 g
- Carbohydrates 0.5 g
- Sugar 0.1 g
- Protein 18.1 g
- Cholesterol 69 mg

Chapter 5: Fish & Seafood

Delicious Shrimp

Preparation Time 10 minutes
Cooking Time 8 minutes
Serve 4

Ingredients:

- 1 lb shrimp, peeled & deveined
- 1/4 tsp garlic powder
- 1/2 tsp chili lime seasoning
- Pepper
- Salt

Directions:

1. Preheat the air fryer to 400 F.
2. Add shrimp, garlic powder, chili lime seasoning, pepper, and salt into the bowl and toss well.
3. Spray air fryer basket with cooking spray.
4. Add shrimp to the air fryer basket and cook for 6-8 minutes.
5. Serve and enjoy.

Nutritional Value (Amount per Serving):

- Calories 137
- Fat 1.9 g
- Carbohydrates 1.9 g
- Sugar 0 g
- Protein 26.1 g
- Cholesterol 239 mg

Delicious Crab Patties

Preparation Time 10 minutes
Cooking Time 10 minutes
Serve 6

Ingredients:

- 2 eggs, lightly beaten
- 2 tbsp fresh lemon juice
- 2 tbsp Greek yogurt
- 2 tbsp green onions, minced
- 3/4 cup breadcrumbs
- 16 oz lump crab meat
- Pepper
- Salt

Directions:

1. Preheat the air fryer to 370 F.
2. Add all ingredients into the bowl and mix until well combined.
3. Spray air fryer basket with cooking spray.
4. Make small patties from mixture and place in air fryer basket and cook for 10 minutes.
5. Serve and enjoy.

Nutritional Value (Amount per Serving):

- Calories 131
- Fat 9.7 g
- Carbohydrates 14 g
- Sugar 3.8 g
- Protein 21.4 g
- Cholesterol 101 mg

Juicy & Flaky Salmon

Preparation Time 10 minutes
Cooking Time 7 minutes
Serve 2

Ingredients:

- 1 1/2 lbs salmon fillets
- 2 tbsp hot sauce
- 3 tbsp honey
- Pepper
- Salt

Directions:

1. In a large bowl, mix hot sauce, honey, pepper, and salt.
2. Add salmon fillets into the bowl and coat with sauce and let it marinate for 30 minutes.
3. Preheat the air fryer to 400 F.
4. Spray air fryer basket with cooking spray.
5. Place salmon in air fryer basket and cook for 7 minutes.
6. Serve and enjoy.

Nutritional Value (Amount per Serving):

- Calories 547
- Fat 21.1 g
- Carbohydrates 26.2 g
- Sugar 26.1 g
- Protein 66.2 g
- Cholesterol 150 mg

Quick & Juicy Tilapia

Preparation Time 10 minutes
Cooking Time 8 minutes
Serve 1

Ingredients:

- 6 oz tilapia fillet
- 1 tsp Italian seasoning
- 1 tbsp parmesan cheese, grated
- 1 tbsp butter, melted
- 1/8 tsp garlic powder
- Pepper
- Salt

Directions:

1. Preheat the air fryer to 400 F.
2. Spray air fryer basket with cooking spray.
3. Season fish fillet with garlic powder, pepper, and salt.
4. Place the fish fillet in an air fryer basket and cook for 8 minutes. Flip fish halfway through.
5. In a small bowl, mix butter, cheese, and Italian seasoning.
6. Place a fish fillet on a plate and drizzle with butter mixture.
7. Serve and enjoy.

Nutritional Value (Amount per Serving):

- Calories 348
- Fat 20.4 g
- Carbohydrates 1.8 g
- Sugar 0.5 g
- Protein 40.9 g
- Cholesterol 137 mg

Quick & Spicy Scallops

Preparation Time 10 minutes
Cooking Time 6 minutes
Serve 2

Ingredients:

- 6 sea scallops
- 1/2 tsp Cajun seasoning
- Pepper
- Salt

Directions:

1. Preheat the air fryer to 400 F.
2. Spray air fryer basket with cooking spray.
3. In a bowl, toss scallops with Cajun seasoning, pepper, and salt.
4. Add scallops to the air fryer basket and cook for 6 minutes. Flip scallops halfway through.
5. Serve and enjoy.

Nutritional Value (Amount per Serving):

- Calories 79
- Fat 0.7 g
- Carbohydrates 2.2 g
- Sugar 0 g
- Protein 15.1 g
- Cholesterol 30 mg

Flavors Blackened Salmon

Preparation Time 10 minutes
Cooking Time 10 minutes
Serve 2

Ingredients:

- 1/2 lb salmon fillets
- 1/2 tbsp olive oil
- 1/2 tbsp blackened seasoning

Directions:

1. Preheat the air fryer to 400 F.
2. Brush fish fillets with oil and sprinkle with seasoning.
3. Place fish fillets in an air fryer basket and cook for 10 minutes.
4. Serve and enjoy.

Nutritional Value (Amount per Serving):

- Calories 180
- Fat 10.5 g
- Carbohydrates 0 g
- Sugar 0 g
- Protein 22 g
- Cholesterol 50 mg

Asian Salmon

Preparation Time 10 minutes
Cooking Time 12 minutes
Serve 2

Ingredients:

- 2 salmon fillets
- 2 tbsp olive oil
- 1/2 tsp garlic, minced
- 3 tbsp honey
- 4 tbsp teriyaki

Directions:

1. Add oil, garlic, honey, and teriyaki into the mixing bowl and mix well.
2. Add fish fillets into the bowl and coat well and allow to marinate for 30 minutes.
3. Place marinated fish fillets in an air fryer basket and air fry at 350 F for 12 minutes. Flip fish fillets halfway through.
4. Serve and enjoy.

Nutritional Value (Amount per Serving):

- Calories 492
- Fat 25 g
- Carbohydrates 36.2 g
- Sugar 33.9 g
- Protein 34.7 g
- Cholesterol 78 mg

Moist & Crisp Cod

Preparation Time 10 minutes
Cooking Time 16 minutes
Serve 6

Ingredients:

- 1 1/2 lbs cod fillets
- 1/2 tsp garlic powder
- 1 tsp paprika
- 2 tsp old bay seasoning
- 3/4 cup flour
- 1/8 tsp salt

Directions:

1. Preheat the air fryer to 360 F.
2. Spray air fryer basket with cooking spray.
3. In a shallow dish, mix flour, old bay seasoning, paprika, garlic powder, and salt.
4. Coat fish fillets with flour mixture and place in air fryer basket and cook for 16 minutes. Flip fish fillets halfway through.
5. Serve and enjoy.

Nutritional Value (Amount per Serving):

- Calories 150
- Fat 1.2 g
- Carbohydrates 13.3 g
- Sugar 0.1 g
- Protein 22 g
- Cholesterol 56 mg

Asian Shrimp

Preparation Time 10 minutes
Cooking Time 6 minutes
Serve 6

Ingredients:

- 2 lbs shrimp, peeled & deveined
- 1 tsp garlic, minced
- 1 tbsp fresh lemon juice
- 2 tbsp gochujang
- 2 tbsp honey
- 2 tbsp soy sauce
- 1 tbsp olive oil
- Pepper
- Salt

Directions:

1. Add shrimp and remaining ingredients into the mixing bowl and mix well and allow to marinate for 30 minutes.
2. Preheat the air fryer to 350 F.
3. Spray air fryer basket with cooking spray.
4. Place shrimp into the air fryer basket and cook for 6 minutes.
5. Serve and enjoy.

Nutritional Value (Amount per Serving):

- Calories 230
- Fat 4.9 g
- Carbohydrates 9.9 g
- Sugar 6.6 g
- Protein 35 g
- Cholesterol 318 mg

Lemon Butter Cod

Preparation Time 10 minutes
Cooking Time 10 minutes
Serve 4

Ingredients:

- 4 cod fillets
- 1 tsp dried dill
- 2 tbsp fresh lemon juice
- 1 tbsp garlic, minced
- 1/4 cup butter, melted
- 1/2 tsp salt

Directions:

1. Preheat the air fryer to 350 F.
2. Add dill, lemon juice, garlic, butter, and salt into the mixing bowl and mix well. Add fish fillets and coat well.
3. Place fish fillets into the air fryer basket and cook for 10 minutes.
4. Serve and enjoy.

Nutritional Value (Amount per Serving):

- Calories 197
- Fat 12.6 g
- Carbohydrates 1 g
- Sugar 0.2 g
- Protein 20.4 g
- Cholesterol 86 mg

Crispy Salmon Patties

Preparation Time 10 minutes
Cooking Time 15 minutes
Serve 2

Ingredients:

- 1 egg
- 10 oz can salmon
- 1 tsp dried dill
- 1 green onion, chopped
- 4 tbsp breadcrumbs
- 1/4 tsp garlic powder
- Pepper
- Salt

Directions:

1. Preheat the air fryer to 400 F.
2. Add all ingredients into the bowl and mix until well combined.
3. Spray air fryer basket with cooking spray.
4. Make patties from mixture and place in air fryer basket and cook for 15 minutes.
5. Serve and enjoy.

Nutritional Value (Amount per Serving):

- Calories 287
- Fat 11.5 g
- Carbohydrates 11 g
- Sugar 1.3 g
- Protein 32.9 g
- Cholesterol 160 mg

Spicy Salmon Fillets

Preparation Time: 10 minutes
Cooking Time: 7 minutes
Serve: 2

Ingredients:

- 2 salmon fillets
- 2 tsp olive oil
- 1/8 tsp cayenne
- 2 tsp paprika
- Pepper
- Salt

Directions:

1. Preheat the air fryer to 390 F.
2. Brush fish fillets with oil and sprinkle with cayenne, paprika, pepper, and salt.
3. Place fillets in an air fryer basket and cook for 7 minutes.
4. Serve and enjoy.

Nutritional Value (Amount per Serving):

- Calories 282
- Fat 16 g
- Carbohydrates 1.3 g
- Sugar 0.2 g
- Protein 34.9 g
- Cholesterol 78 mg

Lemon Pepper White Fish Fillets

Preparation Time: 10 minutes
Cooking Time: 10 minutes
Serve: 2

Ingredients:

- 2 white fish fillets
- 1/4 tsp lemon pepper seasoning
- 2 tbsp parmesan cheese
- 2 tbsp coconut flour
- 1/4 tsp garlic powder
- 1 tbsp olive oil

Directions:

1. Preheat the air fryer to 400 F.
2. In a shallow dish, mix coconut flour, garlic powder, cheese, and lemon pepper seasoning.
3. Brush fish fillets with oil and coat with coconut flour mixture.
4. Place fish fillets in an air fryer basket and cook for 10 minutes.
5. Serve and enjoy.

Nutritional Value (Amount per Serving):

- Calories 417
- Fat 25.3 g
- Carbohydrates 6.4 g
- Sugar 0.1 g
- Protein 47.8 g
- Cholesterol 139 mg

Marinated Asian Salmon

Preparation Time: 10 minutes
Cooking Time: 12 minutes
Serve: 2

Ingredients:

- 2 salmon fillets
- 1 tsp sesame seeds, toasted
- 1/2 tsp sriracha sauce
- 3 tbsp coconut aminos
- 1/2 tsp garlic, minced
- 1 tsp ginger, grated

Directions:

1. Preheat the air fryer to 400 F.
2. Add salmon fillets into the zip-lock bag. Mix together the remaining ingredients and pour over fish fillets. Seal bag and place in the fridge for 30 minutes.
3. Place marinated salmon fillets in an air fryer basket and cook for 12 minutes. Flip fish fillets halfway through.
4. Serve and enjoy.

Nutritional Value (Amount per Serving):

- Calories 257
- Fat 12.6 g
- Carbohydrates 5.8 g
- Sugar 0.1 g
- Protein 34.9 g
- Cholesterol 79 mg

Curried Cod

Preparation Time: 10 minutes
Cooking Time: 10 minutes
Serve: 2

Ingredients:

- 2 cod fillets
- 1/8 tsp garlic powder
- 1/8 tsp smoked paprika
- 1/4 tsp curry powder
- 1 tbsp butter, melted
- 1/8 tsp sea salt

Directions:

1. Preheat the air fryer to 360 F.
2. In a small bowl, mix curry powder, garlic powder, paprika, and salt and set aside.
3. Brush fish fillets with butter and rub with spice mixture.
4. Place fish fillets in an air fryer basket and cook for 10 minutes.
5. Serve and enjoy.

Nutritional Value (Amount per Serving):

- Calories 53
- Fat 6.8 g
- Carbohydrates 0.4 g
- Sugar 0.1 g
- Protein 20.1 g
- Cholesterol 70 mg

Easy Teriyaki Salmon

Preparation Time: 10 minutes
Cooking Time: 8 minutes
Serve: 2

Ingredients:

- 2 salmon fillets
- 1 tsp sesame seeds, toasted
- 1/3 cup teriyaki sauce

Directions:

1. Preheat the air fryer to 400 F.
2. Add salmon fillets and teriyaki sauce into the bowl. Cover and allow to marinate for 20 minutes.
3. Place marinated fish fillets in an air fryer basket and cook for 8 minutes.
4. Sprinkle fish fillets with sesame seeds and serve.

Nutritional Value (Amount per Serving):

- Calories 287
- Fat 11.8 g
- Carbohydrates 7.8 g
- Sugar 6.8 g
- Protein 37.7 g
- Cholesterol 78 mg

Asian Sweet & Spicy Salmon

Preparation Time: 10 minutes
Cooking Time: 12 minutes
Serve: 2

Ingredients:

- 2 salmon fillets
- 1/2 tsp chili powder
- 1/4 tsp turmeric
- 3 tbsp honey
- 1 tsp coriander
- Pepper
- Salt

Directions:

1. Preheat the air fryer to 400 F.
2. In a small bowl, mix honey, turmeric, coriander, chili powder, pepper, and salt.
3. Brush fish fillets with honey mixture and place in an air fryer basket and cook for 12 minutes.
4. Serve and enjoy.

Nutritional Value (Amount per Serving):

- Calories 334
- Fat 11.1 g
- Carbohydrates 26.5 g
- Sugar 25.9 g
- Protein 34.7 g
- Cholesterol 78 mg

Quick Rosemary Shrimp

Preparation Time: 10 minutes
Cooking Time: 10 minutes
Serve: 4

Ingredients:

- 1 lb shrimp, peeled and deveined
- 1/2 tbsp fresh rosemary, chopped
- 1/2 tsp garlic, minced
- 1 tbsp butter, melted
- Pepper
- Salt

Directions:

1. Preheat the air fryer to 375 F.
2. Add shrimp and remaining ingredients in a bowl and toss well.
3. Pour shrimp mixture into the air fryer basket and cook for 10 minutes.
4. Serve and enjoy.

Nutritional Value (Amount per Serving):

- Calories 162
- Fat 4.9 g
- Carbohydrates 2.1 g
- Sugar 0 g
- Protein 25.9 g
- Cholesterol 246 mg

Lemon Garlic Spicy Shrimp

Preparation Time: 10 minutes
Cooking Time: 6 minutes
Serve: 4

Ingredients:

- 1 lb shrimp, peeled & deveined
- 1/2 tsp garlic, minced
- 2 tsp fresh lemon juice
- 1 tsp lemon zest, grated
- 1 tsp steak seasoning
- 2 tsp olive oil
- Pepper
- Salt

Directions:

1. Preheat the air fryer to 375 F.
2. Add shrimp and remaining ingredients into the bowl and toss well.
3. Add shrimp mixture into the air fryer basket and cook for 6 minutes.
4. Serve and enjoy.

Nutritional Value (Amount per Serving):

- Calories 156
- Fat 4.3 g
- Carbohydrates 2 g
- Sugar 0.1 g
- Protein 25.9 g
- Cholesterol 239 mg

Flavorful Shrimp Fajitas

Preparation Time: 10 minutes
Cooking Time: 8 minutes
Serve: 4

Ingredients:

- 1 lb shrimp, peeled and deveined
- 1/2 tsp garlic, minced
- 2 bell pepper, sliced
- 1/8 tsp cayenne
- 1 tbsp olive oil
- 1 onion, sliced
- 1 tsp chili powder
- 1 tsp paprika
- Pepper
- Salt

Directions:

1. Preheat the air fryer to 400 F.
2. Add shrimp and remaining ingredients into the bowl and toss well.
3. Add shrimp mixture into the air fryer basket and cook for 8 minutes. Stir halfway through.
4. Serve and enjoy.

Nutritional Value (Amount per Serving):

- Calories 199
- Fat 5.8 g
- Carbohydrates 9.6 g
- Sugar 4.3 g
- Protein 26.9 g
- Cholesterol 239 mg

Chapter 6: Vegetable & Side Dishes

Sweet Potato Bites

Preparation Time 10 minutes
Cooking Time 25 minutes
Serve 4

Ingredients:

- 3 medium sweet potatoes, peel & cut into cubes
- 1 1/2 tsp cinnamon
- 2 tbsp honey
- 1/8 tsp brown sugar
- 1 tbsp olive oil

Directions:

1. Add sweet potatoes, cinnamon, honey, brown sugar, and oil into the bowl and toss well.
2. Add sweet potatoes into the air fryer basket and cook at 400 F for 20-25 minutes. Stir halfway through.
3. Serve and enjoy.

Nutritional Value (Amount per Serving):

- Calories 197
- Fat 3.7 g
- Carbohydrates 40.8 g
- Sugar 9.3 g
- Protein 1.8 g
- Cholesterol 0 mg

Spicy Brussel Sprouts

Preparation Time 10 minutes
Cooking Time 20 minutes
Serve 6

Ingredients:

- 1 lb Brussel sprouts, cut in half
- 1 tsp sesame oil
- 1 tsp vinegar
- 1/4 cup sriracha sauce
- 1/3 cup honey
- 2 tbsp olive oil
- Pepper
- Salt

Directions:

1. In a small bowl, mix sriracha sauce, sesame oil, vinegar, and honey and set aside.
2. Preheat the air fryer to 350 F.
3. In a bowl, toss Brussel sprouts with olive oil, pepper, and salt.
4. Add Brussel sprouts into the air fryer basket and cook for 14 minutes. Stir halfway through.
5. Once done, transfer Brussel sprouts into the mixing bowl. Pour sriracha sauce mixture over sprouts and toss well.
6. Serve and enjoy.

Nutritional Value (Amount per Serving):

- Calories 203
- Fat 12.4 g
- Carbohydrates 23.1 g
- Sugar 17.8 g
- Protein 2.6 g
- Cholesterol 7 mg

Crispy Sugar Snap Peas

Preparation Time 10 minutes
Cooking Time 8 minutes
Serve 4

Ingredients:

- 5 cups sugar snap peas
- 1/4 cup parmesan cheese, shredded
- 1 tsp olive oil
- Pepper
- Salt

Directions:

1. Preheat the air fryer to 400 F.
2. In a bowl, toss sugar snap peas with oil, pepper, and salt.
3. Add sugar snap peas into the air fryer basket and cook for 7 minutes.
4. Sprinkle with shredded cheese and cook for 1 minute more.
5. Serve and enjoy.

Nutritional Value (Amount per Serving):

- Calories 49
- Fat 1.7 g
- Carbohydrates 6 g
- Sugar 3.2 g
- Protein 2.8 g
- Cholesterol 1 mg

Perfect Green Beans

Preparation Time 10 minutes
Cooking Time 8 minutes
Serve 2

Ingredients:

- 1 lb green beans, ends trimmed
- 1/4 tsp garlic powder
- 1 tsp olive oil
- Pepper
- Salt

Directions:

1. Preheat the air fryer to 400 F.
2. Toss green beans with garlic powder, oil, pepper, and salt.
3. Add green beans into the air fryer basket and cook for 8 minutes.
4. Serve and enjoy.

Nutritional Value (Amount per Serving):

- Calories 92
- Fat 2.6 g
- Carbohydrates 16.5 g
- Sugar 3.3 g
- Protein 4.2 g
- Cholesterol 0 mg

Mushroom with Beans & Onions

Preparation Time 10 minutes
Cooking Time 20 minutes
Serve 2

Ingredients:

- 1/2 cup mushrooms, sliced
- 1/2 cup onion, sliced
- 1 1/2 cups green beans, trimmed & cut into pieces
- 2 tsp olive oil
- 1/4 tsp garlic powder
- Pepper
- Salt

Directions:

1. Preheat the air fryer to 375 F.
2. Add mushrooms, onion, green beans, oil, garlic powder, pepper, and salt to the bowl and toss well.
3. Add mushroom mixture into the air fryer basket and cook for 20-25 minutes.
4. Serve and enjoy.

Nutritional Value (Amount per Serving):

- Calories 82
- Fat 4.9 g
- Carbohydrates 9.4 g
- Sugar 2.8 g
- Protein 2.4 g
- Cholesterol 0 mg

Tasty Butternut Squash

Preparation Time 10 minutes
Cooking Time 15 minutes
Serve 4

Ingredients:

- 1 butternut squash, peel & cut into chunks
- 2 tbsp honey
- 1/2 tsp cinnamon
- 2 tbsp olive oil
- 1/4 tsp sea salt

Directions:

1. Preheat the air fryer to 400 F.
2. Add butternut squash, honey, cinnamon, oil, and salt into the bowl and toss well.
3. Add squash into the air fryer basket and cook for 15 minutes. Shake basket 2-3 times.
4. Serve and enjoy.

Nutritional Value (Amount per Serving):

- Calories 108
- Fat 7 g
- Carbohydrates 13 g
- Sugar 9.4 g
- Protein 0.4 g
- Cholesterol 0 mg

Simple Mexican Potatoes

Preparation Time 10 minutes
Cooking Time 15 minutes
Serve 4

Ingredients:

- 2 sweet potatoes, peel & cut into chunks
- 2 tsp fresh lime juice
- 1 tsp cumin
- 1 tbsp chili powder
- 2 tbsp olive oil
- 1/8 tsp cayenne

Directions:

1. Preheat the air fryer to 380 F.
2. Add sweet potatoes and remaining ingredients into the bowl and toss well.
3. Add sweet potatoes into the air fryer basket and cook for 15 minutes or until tender. Shake basket twice.
4. Serve and enjoy.

Nutritional Value (Amount per Serving):

- Calories 162
- Fat 7.6 g
- Carbohydrates 24.1 g
- Sugar 0.9 g
- Protein 1.6 g
- Cholesterol 0 mg

Rosemary Potatoes

Preparation Time 10 minutes
Cooking Time 15 minutes
Serve 4

Ingredients:

- 4 cups baby potatoes, cut into four pieces
- 1 tbsp lemon juice
- 1 tbsp garlic, minced
- 2 tsp dried rosemary, minced
- 3 tbsp olive oil
- Pepper
- Salt

Directions:

1. Preheat the air fryer to 400 F.
2. Add potatoes and remaining ingredients into the bowl and toss well.
3. Add potatoes into the air fryer basket and cook for 15 minutes or until cooked.
4. Serve and enjoy.

Nutritional Value (Amount per Serving):

- Calories 166
- Fat 10.6 g
- Carbohydrates 17.2 g
- Sugar 3.1 g
- Protein 2.2 g
- Cholesterol 0 mg

Tasty Cauliflower Florets

Preparation Time: 10 minutes
Cooking Time: 15 minutes
Serve: 5

Ingredients:

- 1 medium cauliflower head, cut into florets
- 1/2 tsp old bay seasoning
- 1/4 tsp paprika
- 1 tbsp garlic, minced
- 3 tbsp olive oil
- Pepper
- Salt

Directions:

1. Preheat the air fryer to 400 F.
2. In a bowl, toss cauliflower with the remaining ingredients.
3. Add cauliflower florets into the air fryer basket and cook for 15 minutes. Stir halfway through.
4. Serve and enjoy.

Nutritional Value (Amount per Serving):

- Calories 104
- Fat 8 g
- Carbohydrates 6 g
- Sugar 2 g
- Protein 2 g
- Cholesterol 0 mg

Garlic Cauliflower Florets

Preparation Time: 10 minutes
Cooking Time: 20 minutes
Serve: 4

Ingredients:

- 5 cups cauliflower florets
- 6 garlic cloves, chopped
- 4 tablespoons olive oil
- 1/4 tsp chili powder
- 1/2 tsp cumin powder
- 1/2 tsp salt

Directions:

1. Preheat the air fryer to 400 F.
2. Add all ingredients into the bowl and toss well.
3. Add cauliflower florets into the air fryer basket and cook for 20 minutes.
4. Serve and enjoy.

Nutritional Value (Amount per Serving):

- Calories 160
- Fat 14 g
- Carbohydrates 8 g
- Sugar 3 g
- Protein 3 g
- Cholesterol 0 mg

Simple Sweet Potato Fries

Preparation Time: 10 minutes
Cooking Time: 12 minutes
Serve: 2

Ingredients:

- 2 sweet potatoes, peeled and cut into fries shape
- 1/4 tsp chili powder
- 1/8 tsp cayenne
- 1/2 tsp garlic powder
- 1 tbsp olive oil
- Salt

Directions:

1. Preheat the air fryer to 350 F.
2. In a bowl, add sweet potato fries, chili powder, cayenne, garlic powder, olive oil, and salt and toss well.
3. Add sweet potato fries into the air fryer basket and cook for 12 minutes. Stir halfway through.
4. Serve and enjoy.

Nutritional Value (Amount per Serving):

- Calories 241
- Fat 7.4 g
- Carbohydrates 42.6 g
- Sugar 1 g
- Protein 2.5 g
- Cholesterol 0 mg

Healthy Zucchini Patties

Preparation Time: 10 minutes
Cooking Time: 20 minutes
Serve: 6

Ingredients:

- 1 egg, lightly beaten
- 1 cup zucchini, shredded and squeezed
- 1/4 cup parmesan cheese, grated
- 1/2 tbsp Dijon mustard
- 1/2 tbsp mayonnaise
- 1/2 cup breadcrumbs
- 2 tbsp onion, minced
- Pepper
- Salt

Directions:

1. Preheat the air fryer to 375 F.
2. Add all ingredients into the bowl and mix until well combined.
3. Make patties from the zucchini mixture and place them in an air fryer basket and cook for 20 minutes. Turn patties halfway through.
4. Serve and enjoy.

Nutritional Value (Amount per Serving):

- Calories 60
- Fat 2 g
- Carbohydrates 7.9 g
- Sugar 1.2 g
- Protein 2.8 g
- Cholesterol 28 mg

Air Fryer Potatoes & Carrots

Preparation Time: 10 minutes
Cooking Time: 30 minutes
Serve: 2

Ingredients:

- 1/2 lb potatoes, cut into 1-inch cubes
- 1/2 onion, diced
- 1/2 tsp Italian seasoning
- 1/2 lb carrots, peeled & cut into chunks
- 1 tbsp olive oil
- 1/4 tsp garlic powder
- Pepper
- Salt

Directions:

1. Preheat the air fryer to 375 F.
2. In a bowl, add carrots, potatoes, and remaining ingredients and toss well.
3. Transfer carrot potato mixture into the air fryer basket and cook for 30 minutes. Stir halfway through.
4. Serve and enjoy.

Nutritional Value (Amount per Serving):

- Calories 201
- Fat 7.5 g
- Carbohydrates 32 g
- Sugar 8.2 g
- Protein 3.2 g
- Cholesterol 1 mg

Broccoli Fritters

Preparation Time: 10 minutes
Cooking Time: 20 minutes
Serve: 4

Ingredients:

- 2 eggs, lightly beaten
- 3 cups broccoli florets, cooked & mashed
- 2 cups cheddar cheese, shredded
- 1/4 cup breadcrumbs
- 1/2 tsp garlic, minced
- Pepper
- Salt

Directions:

1. Preheat the air fryer to 350 F.
2. Add all ingredients into the bowl and mix until well combined.
3. Make patties from broccoli mixture and place in air fryer basket and cook for 20 minutes. Flip patties halfway through.
4. Serve and enjoy.

Nutritional Value (Amount per Serving):

- Calories 310
- Fat 21.5 g
- Carbohydrates 10.4 g
- Sugar 2 g
- Protein 19.7 g
- Cholesterol 141 mg

Tasty Zucchini & Squash

Preparation Time: 10 minutes
Cooking Time: 15 minutes
Serve: 4

Ingredients:

- 2 zucchini, sliced
- 1 tsp garlic, minced
- 1/4 tsp onion powder
- 1/4 tsp chili powder
- 2 yellow squash, sliced
- 1 tsp olive oil
- Pepper
- Salt

Directions:

1. Preheat the air fryer to 375 F.
2. In a bowl, add squash, zucchini, and remaining ingredients and toss well.
3. Add squash and zucchini mixture into the air fryer basket and cook for 15 minutes. Stir halfway through.
4. Serve and enjoy.

Nutritional Value (Amount per Serving):

- Calories 44
- Fat 1.6 g
- Carbohydrates 7 g
- Sugar 3.5 g
- Protein 2.5 g
- Cholesterol 0 mg

Chapter 7: Snack & Appetizers

Healthy Chicken Meatballs

Preparation Time 10 minutes
Cooking Time 20 minutes
Serve 4

Ingredients:

- 1 lb ground chicken
- 1/2 tsp ground coriander
- 1 tsp fresh ginger, grated
- 1 tsp ground cumin
- 1 1/2 tbsp curry paste
- 2 tbsp fresh mint, chopped
- 1/4 cup bell pepper, chopped
- 1/2 cup onion, chopped
- 1/4 tsp pepper
- 1/2 tsp sea salt

Directions:

1. Preheat the air fryer to 325 F.
2. Spray air fryer basket with cooking spray.
3. Add ground chicken and remaining ingredients into the bowl and mix until well combined.
4. Make small balls from mixture and place in air fryer basket and cook for 20 minutes or until cooked.
5. Serve and enjoy.

Nutritional Value (Amount per Serving):

- Calories 267
- Fat 11.9 g
- Carbohydrates 4.4 g
- Sugar 1 g
- Protein 33.6 g
- Cholesterol 101 mg

Crispy Potato Wedges

Preparation Time 10 minutes
Cooking Time 15 minutes
Serve 6

Ingredients:

- 1 1/2 lbs potatoes, cut into wedges
- 3 tbsp parmesan cheese, grated
- 1/2 tsp chili flakes
- 1/2 tsp dried oregano
- 1 tbsp garlic, minced
- 1 1/2 tbsp olive oil
- 1/4 tsp kosher salt

Directions:

1. Preheat the air fryer to 400 F.
2. Add potato wedges and remaining ingredients into the mixing bowl and toss well.
3. Add potato wedges into the air fryer basket and air fry for 12-15 minutes. Stir halfway through.
4. Serve and enjoy.

Nutritional Value (Amount per Serving):

- Calories 156
- Fat 6.6 g
- Carbohydrates 18.9 g
- Sugar 1.3 g
- Protein 6.5 g
- Cholesterol 10 mg

Delicious BBQ Chickpeas

Preparation Time 10 minutes
Cooking Time 17 minutes
Serve 4

Ingredients:

- 14.5 oz can chickpeas, drained
- 1/4 tsp dry mustard
- 1/2 tsp garlic powder
- 1 tsp brown sugar
- 1 1/2 tsp smoked paprika
- 1/4 tsp pepper
- 1/2 tsp salt

Directions:

1. Preheat the air fryer to 390 F.
2. Add chickpeas into the air fryer basket and air fry for 5 minutes.
3. Spray chickpeas with cooking spray and air fry for 10 minutes more.
4. In a bowl, toss chickpeas with mustard, garlic powder, brown sugar, paprika, pepper, and salt.
5. Return chickpeas to the air fryer basket and air fry for 2 minutes more.
6. Serve and enjoy.

Nutritional Value (Amount per Serving):

- Calories 130
- Fat 1.3 g
- Carbohydrates 24.8 g
- Sugar 0.9 g
- Protein 5.3 g
- Cholesterol 0 mg

Delicious Broccoli Tots

Preparation Time 10 minutes
Cooking Time 12 minutes
Serve 4

Ingredients:

- 1 egg yolk
- 3 tbsp parmesan cheese, grated
- 2 tbsp breadcrumbs
- 3 cups broccoli, cooked & mashed
- 1/4 tsp garlic powder
- Pepper
- Salt

Directions:

1. Preheat the air fryer to 370 F.
2. Add all ingredients into the bowl and mix until well combined.
3. Make small tots from mixture and place in air fryer basket and cook for 10-12 minutes.
4. Serve and enjoy.

Nutritional Value (Amount per Serving):

- Calories 118
- Fat 6 g
- Carbohydrates 8 g
- Sugar 1.4 g
- Protein 9.8 g
- Cholesterol 67 mg

Crispy Apple Fries

Preparation Time: 10 minutes
Cooking Time: 5 minutes
Serve: 2

Ingredients:

- 1 apple, sliced
- 1/2 tsp sugar
- 1/2 tsp cinnamon
- 1 tbsp butter, melted
- 1 tbsp cracker crumbs

Directions:

1. Preheat the air fryer to 400 F.
2. Add apple slices and butter into the bowl and toss well.
3. Add cinnamon, cracker crumbs, and sugar and mix well.
4. Place apple slices into the air fryer basket and cook for 5 minutes.
5. Serve and enjoy.

Nutritional Value (Amount per Serving):

- Calories 124
- Fat 6.5 g
- Carbohydrates 18.1 g
- Sugar 12.6 g
- Protein 0.5 g
- Cholesterol 15 mg

Easy Carrot Fries

Preparation Time: 10 minutes
Cooking Time: 12 minutes
Serve: 4

Ingredients:

- 4 carrots, peeled and cut into fries
- 1/4 tsp chili powder
- 1/4 tsp onion powder
- 2 tbsp parmesan cheese, grated
- 1/2 tsp garlic powder
- 2 tbsp olive oil
- Pepper
- Salt

Directions:

1. Preheat the air fryer to 350 F.
2. Add carrots and remaining ingredients into the bowl and toss well.
3. Spread carrots fries in an air fryer basket and cook for 12 minutes. Stir halfway through.
4. Serve and enjoy.

Nutritional Value (Amount per Serving):

- Calories 132
- Fat 10 g
- Carbohydrates 7 g
- Sugar 3.2 g
- Protein 5.1 g
- Cholesterol 10 mg

Sweet Cinnamon Chickpeas

Preparation Time: 10 minutes
Cooking Time: 12 minutes
Serve: 4

Ingredients:

- 14.5 oz can chickpeas, drained & pat dry
- 1 tbsp butter, melted
- 1/2 tsp cinnamon
- 1 tbsp honey
- Pepper
- Salt

Directions:

1. Preheat the air fryer to 375 F.
2. Add chickpeas into the air fryer basket and cook for 12 minutes. Stir halfway through.
3. In a bowl, mix together cinnamon, honey, oil, pepper, and salt.
4. Add chickpeas and toss well.
5. Serve and enjoy.

Nutritional Value (Amount per Serving):

- Calories 165
- Fat 4.1 g
- Carbohydrates 27.8 g
- Sugar 4.3 g
- Protein 5.2 g
- Cholesterol 8 mg

Crispy Veggies

Preparation Time: 10 minutes
Cooking Time: 18 minutes
Serve: 4

Ingredients:

- 1 cup cauliflower, cut into florets
- 1 cup carrots, sliced
- 1 cup broccoli florets
- 1/4 tsp chili powder
- 1/4 tsp onion powder
- 1 tbsp olive oil
- 1/2 tsp garlic powder
- Pepper
- Salt

Directions:

1. Preheat the air fryer to 380 F.
2. Add all vegetables and remaining ingredients into the bowl and toss well.
3. Transfer vegetables to an air fryer basket and cook for 18 minutes. Stir halfway through.
4. Serve and enjoy.

Nutritional Value (Amount per Serving):

- Calories 58
- Fat 3.6 g
- Carbohydrates 6 g
- Sugar 2.5 g
- Protein 1.5 g
- Cholesterol 0 mg

Air Fryer Pecans

Preparation Time: 10 minutes
Cooking Time: 6 minutes
Serve: 4

Ingredients:

- 1 cup pecan halves
- 1/4 tsp chili powder
- 1 tbsp butter, melted
- Pepper
- Salt

Directions:

1. Preheat the air fryer to 200 F.
2. Add pecans, chili powder, butter, and salt in a bowl and toss well.
3. Transfer pecans to an air fryer basket and cook for 6 minutes. Stir halfway through.
4. Serve and enjoy.

Nutritional Value (Amount per Serving):

- Calories 130
- Fat 13.6 g
- Carbohydrates 2.3 g
- Sugar 0.6 g
- Protein 1.7 g
- Cholesterol 8 mg

Rosemary Basil Mushrooms

Preparation Time: 10 minutes
Cooking Time: 14 minutes
Serve: 4

Ingredients:

- 1 lb mushroom
- 1/2 tsp garlic, minced
- 1/2 tbsp vinegar
- 1 tsp rosemary, chopped
- 1/4 tsp chili powder
- 1 tbsp basil, minced
- Pepper
- Salt

Directions:

1. Preheat the air fryer to 350 F.
2. Add all ingredients into the large bowl and toss well.
3. Add mushrooms to an air fryer basket and cook for 14 minutes. Stir halfway through.
4. Serve and enjoy.

Nutritional Value (Amount per Serving):

- Calories 27
- Fat 0.4 g
- Carbohydrates 4.2 g
- Sugar 2 g
- Protein 3.6 g
- Cholesterol 0 mg

Savory & Healthy Almonds

Preparation Time: 10 minutes
Cooking Time: 8 minutes
Serve: 4

Ingredients:

- 1 cup almonds
- 1/4 tsp chili powder
- 1/2 tbsp soy sauce
- 1/2 tsp paprika
- 1/2 tbsp garlic powder
- Salt

Directions:

1. Preheat the air fryer to 320 F.
2. Add paprika, chili powder, garlic powder, and soy sauce in a bowl and stir well. Add almonds and mix well.
3. Add almonds into the air fryer basket and cook for 8 minutes.
4. Serve and enjoy.

Nutritional Value (Amount per Serving):

- Calories 143
- Fat 12 g
- Carbohydrates 6.2 g
- Sugar 1.3 g
- Protein 5.4 g
- Cholesterol 0 mg

Crispy Eggplant Slices

Preparation Time: 10 minutes
Cooking Time: 20 minutes
Serve: 4

Ingredients:

- 1 eggplant, cut into 1-inch slices
- 1/2 tsp chili powder
- 1 tsp garlic powder
- 1/8 tsp cayenne
- 1 tsp paprika
- 2 tbsp olive oil
- Pepper
- Salt

Directions:

1. Preheat the air fryer to 375 F.
2. Add all ingredients into the bowl and toss well.
3. Place eggplant slices in an air fryer basket and cook for 20 minutes. Flip eggplant slices halfway through.
4. Serve and enjoy.

Nutritional Value (Amount per Serving):

- Calories 94
- Fat 7.4 g
- Carbohydrates 7.8 g
- Sugar 3.7 g
- Protein 1.4 g
- Cholesterol 0 mg

Healthy Turkey Patties

Preparation Time: 10 minutes
Cooking Time: 10 minutes
Serve: 4

Ingredients:

- 1 lb ground turkey
- 1 tsp garlic, grated
- 1 tbsp onion, grated
- 1/4 cup breadcrumbs
- 6 oz zucchini, grated
- 1/4 tsp chili powder
- Pepper
- Salt

Directions:

1. Preheat the air fryer to 370 F.
2. Add ground turkey and remaining ingredients into the bowl and mix until well combined.
3. Make patties from the mixture and place them in the air fryer basket and cook for 10 minutes. Turn patties halfway through.
4. Serve and enjoy.

Nutritional Value (Amount per Serving):

- Calories 257
- Fat 12.9 g
- Carbohydrates 6.9 g
- Sugar 1.3 g
- Protein 32.5 g
- Cholesterol 116 mg

Cripsy Chicken Wings

Preparation Time: 10 minutes
Cooking Time: 30 minutes
Serve: 4

Ingredients:

- 1 lb chicken wings
- 3/4 tsp taco seasoning
- 1 tsp olive oil
- Pepper
- Salt

Directions:

1. Preheat the air fryer to 400 F.
2. In a bowl, add chicken wings, taco seasoning, oil, pepper, and salt, and toss well to coat.
3. Place chicken wings in an air fryer basket and cook for 30 minutes. Turn chicken wings halfway through.
4. Serve and enjoy.

Nutritional Value (Amount per Serving):

- Calories 228
- Fat 9.7 g
- Carbohydrates 0.2 g
- Sugar 0 g
- Protein 33 g
- Cholesterol 101 mg

Tasty Chicken Patties

Preparation Time: 10 minutes
Cooking Time: 14 minutes
Serve: 2

Ingredients:

- 8 oz ground chicken
- 2 tsp fresh oregano, chopped
- 1/4 tsp chili powder
- 1/4 tsp poultry seasoning
- 1 1/2 tbsp olive oil
- 1/2 tsp garlic, minced
- 1/4 tsp salt

Directions:

1. Preheat the air fryer to 360 F.
2. Add ground chicken and remaining ingredients into the bowl and mix until well combined.
3. Make patties from the mixture and place them in the air fryer basket and cook for 14 minutes. Turn patties halfway through.
4. Serve and enjoy.

Nutritional Value (Amount per Serving):

- Calories 313
- Fat 19.1 g
- Carbohydrates 1.5 g
- Sugar 0.1 g
- Protein 33.1 g
- Cholesterol 101 mg

Crispy Chicken Nuggets

Preparation Time: 10 minutes
Cooking Time: 12 minutes
Serve: 4

Ingredients:

- 1 egg, lightly beaten
- 1 lb chicken breasts, boneless & cut into 1-inch pieces
- 1 cup breadcrumbs
- 1 tsp Italian seasoning
- 2 tsp sea salt

Directions:

1. Preheat the air fryer to 400 F.
2. Add egg in a shallow bowl.
3. In a shallow dish, mix breadcrumbs, Italian seasoning, and salt.
4. Dip chicken pieces in egg then coat with breadcrumb mixture.
5. Place coated chicken pieces in an air fryer basket and cook for 12 minutes. Flip chicken nuggets halfway through.
6. Serve and enjoy.

Nutritional Value (Amount per Serving):

- Calories 341
- Fat 11.3 g
- Carbohydrates 19.6 g
- Sugar 1.9 g
- Protein 37.8 g
- Cholesterol 143 mg

Tasty Chicken Tenders

Preparation Time: 10 minutes
Cooking Time: 13 minutes
Serve: 4

Ingredients:

- 6 chicken tenders
- 1 tsp oregano
- 1 tsp garlic powder
- 1 tsp smoked paprika
- 1/4 tsp pepper
- 1 tsp kosher salt

Directions:

1. Preheat the air fryer to 380 F.
2. In a small bowl, mix together oregano, garlic powder, smoked paprika, pepper, and salt and rub all over chicken tenders.
3. Place chicken tenders in an air fryer basket and cook for 13 minutes. Turn chicken tenders halfway through.
4. Serve and enjoy.

Nutritional Value (Amount per Serving):

- Calories 421
- Fat 16.4 g
- Carbohydrates 1.1 g
- Sugar 0.2 g
- Protein 63.6 g
- Cholesterol 195 mg

Crispy Burger Patties

Preparation Time: 10 minutes
Cooking Time: 10 minutes
Serve: 4

Ingredients:

- 1 lb ground turkey
- 1 onion, chopped
- 4 oz mushrooms, chopped
- 1/4 cup breadcrumbs
- 1 tbsp soy sauce
- 1 tsp garlic, minced
- Pepper
- Salt

Directions:

1. Preheat the air fryer to 330 F.
2. Add mushrooms into the food processor and process until finely chopped.
3. In a bowl, add ground turkey, mushroom, and remaining ingredients and mix until well combined.
4. Make patties from mixture and place in air fryer basket and cook for 10 minutes.
5. Serve and enjoy.

Nutritional Value (Amount per Serving):

- Calories 268
- Fat 12.9 g
- Carbohydrates 8.9 g
- Sugar 2.2 g
- Protein 33.4 g
- Cholesterol 116 mg

Tasty Eggplant Chunks

Preparation Time: 10 minutes
Cooking Time: 12 minutes
Serve: 2

Ingredients:

- 1 eggplant, cut into chunks
- 1/2 tsp garlic powder
- 1/4 tsp paprika
- 1/4 tsp oregano
- 1 tbsp olive oil

Directions:

1. Preheat the air fryer to 390 F.
2. Add all ingredients into the bowl and toss well.
3. Transfer eggplant into the air fryer basket and cook for 12 minutes. Stir halfway through.
4. Serve and enjoy.

Nutritional Value (Amount per Serving):

- Calories 121
- Fat 7.5 g
- Carbohydrates 14.2 g
- Sugar 7.1 g
- Protein 2.4 g
- Cholesterol 0 mg

Flavorful Okra

Preparation Time: 10 minutes
Cooking Time: 10 minutes
Serve: 2

Ingredients:

- 3 cups okra, wash & dry
- 1 tsp cumin powder
- 1 tsp chili powder
- 1/8 tsp dry mango powder
- 3 tbsp gram flour
- Salt

Directions:

1. Preheat the air fryer to 390 F.
2. Using a knife make a horizontal cut in each okra and set it aside.
3. In a bowl, mix gram flour, mango powder, chili powder, cumin powder, and salt.
4. Add little water and make a thick batter.
5. Fill the batter in each okra and place it in an air fryer basket and cook for 10 minutes.
6. Serve and enjoy.

Nutritional Value (Amount per Serving):

- Calories 103
- Fat 1.3 g
- Carbohydrates 17.8 g
- Sugar 3.6 g
- Protein 5.2 g
- Cholesterol 0 mg

Chapter 8: Desserts

Moist Banana Muffins

Preparation Time: 10 minutes
Cooking Time: 15 minutes
Serve: 10

Ingredients:

- 1 egg
- 2 very ripe bananas
- 3/4 cup self-raising flour
- 1 tsp cinnamon
- 1 tsp vanilla
- 1/2 cup brown sugar
- 1/3 cup olive oil

Directions:

1. Preheat the air fryer to 320 F.
2. In a bowl, mash the bananas, then add egg, vanilla, oil, and brown sugar and mix until well combined.
3. Add cinnamon and flour and mix until just combined.
4. Pour batter into the 10 silicone muffin molds.
5. Place muffin molds into the air fryer basket and cook for 15 minutes.
6. Serve and enjoy.

Nutritional Value (Amount per Serving):

- Calories 148
- Fat 7.3 g
- Carbohydrates 19 g
- Sugar 10 g
- Protein 1.8 g
- Cholesterol 16 mg

Chocolate Cake

Preparation Time: 10 minutes
Cooking Time: 10 minutes
Serve: 4

Ingredients:

- 2 eggs
- 1 1/2 tbsp self-rising flour
- 3 1/2 tbsp sugar
- 1 cup dark chocolate, chopped
- 6 tbsp butter
- 1 tsp vanilla

Directions:

1. Preheat the air fryer to 370 F.
2. In a bowl, melt butter and chocolate. Stir well.
3. In a separate bowl, whisk eggs with sugar and vanilla.
4. Add melted chocolate and flour and stir until smooth.
5. Pour mixture into the four greased ramekins.
6. Place ramekins in air fryer basket and cook for 10 minutes.
7. Serve and enjoy.

Nutritional Value (Amount per Serving):

- Calories 462
- Fat 32 g
- Carbohydrates 38 g
- Sugar 32 g
- Protein 6 g
- Cholesterol 137 mg

Easy Apple Crisp

Preparation Time: 10 minutes
Cooking Time: 25 minutes
Serve: 1

Ingredients:

- 1 apple, peel, cored & diced
- 1/8 tsp cinnamon
- 1/2 tsp sugar
- For topping:
- 2 tbsp butter
- 1/2 tsp cinnamon
- 2 tsp all-purpose flour
- 2 tbsp sugar

Directions:

1. Preheat the air fryer to 350 F.
2. Add apple, cinnamon, and sugar in greased ramekin and mix well.
3. Mix together all topping ingredients and add on top of the apple mixture.
4. Place ramekin in air fryer basket and cook for 25 minutes.
5. Serve and enjoy.

Nutritional Value (Amount per Serving):

- Calories 440
- Fat 23 g
- Carbohydrates 62 g
- Sugar 49 g
- Protein 1.4 g
- Cholesterol 61 mg

Peanut Butter Cookies

Preparation Time: 10 minutes
Cooking Time: 7 minutes
Serve: 8

Ingredients:

- 1 egg
- 2 tbsp milk
- 1/2 cup sugar
- 1/2 cup brown sugar
- 1/2 cup peanut butter, smooth
- 1/2 cup butter, softened
- 3/4 tsp baking soda
- 1 3/4 cup all-purpose flour
- 1/2 tsp salt

Directions:

1. Preheat the air fryer to 350 F.
2. In a bowl, beat butter and peanut butter using a hand mixer until smooth.
3. Add sugar, brown sugar, milk, and egg, and beat well.
4. Add flour, baking soda, and salt and mix until combined.
5. Make cookies from mixture and place in air fryer basket and cook for 7 minutes.
6. Serve and enjoy.

Nutritional Value (Amount per Serving):

- Calories 387
- Fat 20 g
- Carbohydrates 45 g
- Sugar 23 g
- Protein 7 g
- Cholesterol 51 mg

Choco Chip Cookies

Preparation Time: 10 minutes
Cooking Time: 10 minutes
Serve: 8

Ingredients:

- 1 egg
- 1/2 cup chocolate chips
- 1/4 tsp baking powder
- 1/4 tsp baking soda
- 3/4 cup all-purpose flour
- 1/2 tsp vanilla
- 1/4 cup sugar
- 1/4 cup brown sugar
- 1/4 cup butter, softened
- 1/4 tsp salt

Directions:

1. Preheat the air fryer to 300 F.
2. In a bowl, beat butter, sugar, and brown sugar until smooth.
3. Add egg and vanilla and beat well.
4. Add baking powder, baking soda, flour, chocolate chips, and salt and mix until well combined.
5. Make cookies from mixture and place in air fryer basket and cook for 10 minutes.
6. Serve and enjoy.

Nutritional Value (Amount per Serving):

- Calories 199
- Fat 9.5 g
- Carbohydrates 26 g
- Sugar 16 g
- Protein 2.8 g
- Cholesterol 38 mg

Cinnamon Bagel Bites

Preparation Time: 10 minutes
Cooking Time: 10 minutes
Serve: 2

Ingredients:

- 1/2 cup whole wheat flour
- 2 tsp butter
- 1/2 cup Greek yogurt
- 3/4 tsp baking powder
- 1/2 tsp cinnamon
- 1 packet Truvia
- 1/8 tsp salt

Directions:

1. Preheat the air fryer to 360 F.
2. Add all ingredients into the bowl and mix until well combined.
3. Make small balls from mixture and place in air fryer basket and cook for 10 minutes.
4. Serve and enjoy.

Nutritional Value (Amount per Serving):

- Calories 151
- Fat 4 g
- Carbohydrates 25 g
- Sugar 0.1 g
- Protein 3.3 g
- Cholesterol 10 mg

Chocolate Donuts

Preparation Time: 10 minutes
Cooking Time: 10 minutes
Serve: 8

Ingredients:

- 1 egg
- 1 cup all-purpose flour
- 1 tsp vanilla
- 2 tbsp butter, melted
- 1/2 cup sugar
- 1/2 cup buttermilk
- 1/2 tsp baking soda
- 1/4 cup cocoa powder
- 1/8 tsp salt

Directions:

1. Preheat the air fryer to 350 F.
2. In a bowl, whisk egg, vanilla, butter, and buttermilk.
3. Add remaining ingredients and mix until well combined.
4. Pour batter into the silicone donut molds.
5. Place molds in air fryer basket and cook for 10 minutes.
6. Serve and enjoy.

Nutritional Value (Amount per Serving):

- Calories 151
- Fat 4 g
- Carbohydrates 26 g
- Sugar 13 g
- Protein 3 g
- Cholesterol 29 mg

Brownie Muffins

Preparation Time: 10 minutes
Cooking Time: 15 minutes
Serve: 6

Ingredients:

- 1 egg
- 3/4 cup all-purpose flour
- 1/3 cup chocolate chips
- 1/2 tsp baking powder
- 1/4 cup cocoa powder
- 1/2 tsp vanilla
- 1/2 cup sugar
- 1/2 cup butter, melted
- 1/4 tsp salt

Directions:

1. Preheat the air fryer to 350 F.
2. In a bowl, whisk egg, vanilla, sugar, and butter.
3. Add remaining ingredients and mix until well combined.
4. Pour batter into the silicone muffin molds.
5. Place muffin molds into the air fryer basket and cook for 15 minutes.
6. Serve and enjoy.

Nutritional Value (Amount per Serving):

- Calories 325
- Fat 19 g
- Carbohydrates 36 g
- Sugar 21 g
- Protein 4 g
- Cholesterol 70 mg

Almond Flour Muffins

Preparation Time: 10 minutes
Cooking Time: 15 minutes
Serve: 10

Ingredients:

- 3 eggs
- 1 tsp baking powder
- 1/2 tbsp cinnamon
- 2 cups almond flour
- 1 tsp vanilla
- 2 tbsp butter, melted
- 1/3 cup maple syrup
- 1/4 tsp salt

Directions:

1. Preheat the air fryer to 325 F.
2. In a bowl, whisk eggs, vanilla, butter, and maple syrup.
3. Add remaining ingredients and mix until well combined.
4. Pour batter into the silicone muffin molds.
5. Place muffin molds into the air fryer basket and cook for 15 minutes.
6. Serve and enjoy.

Nutritional Value (Amount per Serving):

- Calories 197
- Fat 14 g
- Carbohydrates 12 g
- Sugar 7 g
- Protein 6 g
- Cholesterol 55 mg

Lemon Muffins

Preparation Time: 10 minutes
Cooking Time: 15 minutes
Serve: 8

Ingredients:

- 1 egg
- 1 cup all-purpose flour
- 1/4 tsp baking soda
- 1 tsp baking powder
- 2 tsp lemon zest
- 1/4 cup butter, melted
- 1/4 cup milk
- 1/2 cup sugar
- 2 tsp chia seeds
- 1/4 tsp salt

Directions:

1. Preheat the air fryer to 325 F.
2. In a bowl, whisk egg, milk, butter, and sugar.
3. Add remaining ingredients and mix until well combined.
4. Pour batter into the silicone muffin molds.
5. Place muffin molds into the air fryer basket and cook for 15 minutes.
6. Serve and enjoy.

Nutritional Value (Amount per Serving):

- Calories 167
- Fat 6 g
- Carbohydrates 25 g
- Sugar 13 g
- Protein 2 g
- Cholesterol 36 mg

Chapter 9: 30-Day Meal Plan

Day 1

Breakfast-Savory & Crispy Hash Browns

Lunch- Juicy Turkey Breast

Dinner- Dijon Lamb Chops

Day 2

Breakfast-Sweet Potato with Cranberries

Lunch- Juicy & Flaky Salmon

Dinner- Simple & Delicious Pork Chops

Day 3

Breakfast-Cheese Omelet

Lunch- Flavorful Chicken Fajitas

Dinner- Air fryer Pork ribs

Day 4

Breakfast-Zucchini Egg Muffins

Lunch- Quick & Juicy Tilapia

Dinner- Dijon Lamb Chops

Day 5

Breakfast-Greek Egg Muffins

Lunch- Easy BBQ Chicken

Dinner- Brined Pork Chops

Day 6

Breakfast-Crispy Breakfast Potatoes

Lunch- Flavors Blackened Salmon

Dinner- Marinated Pork Chops

Day 7

Breakfast-Herb Egg Breakfast Muffins

Lunch- Healthy Greek Chicken

Dinner- Tender & Juicy Pork Chops

Day 8

Breakfast-Cheese Egg Bake

Lunch- Asian Salmon

Dinner- Flavorful Steak Bites

Day 9

Breakfast-Italian Egg Muffins

Lunch- Sesame Chicken

Dinner- Sweet & Juicy Pork Chops

Day 10

Breakfast-Kale Egg Muffins

Lunch- Moist & Crisp Cod

Dinner- Steak Bites

Day 11

Breakfast-Savory & Crispy Hash Browns

Lunch- Tender & Flavorful Chicken Breast

Dinner- Air Fryer Perfect Steak

Day 12

Breakfast-Zucchini Egg Muffins

Lunch- Lemon Butter Cod

Dinner- Delicious Steak Fajitas

Day 13

Breakfast-Kale Egg Muffins

Lunch- Cajun Chicken Thighs

Dinner- Juicy Pork Chops

Day 14

Breakfast- Greek Egg Muffins

Lunch- Spicy Salmon Fillets

Dinner- Sweet & Spicy Pork Chops

Day 15

Breakfast- Cheese Omelet

Lunch- Simple Adobo Chicken

Dinner- Simple & Juicy Pork Chops

Day 16

Breakfast-Savory & Crispy Hash Browns

Lunch- Juicy Turkey Breast

Dinner- Dijon Lamb Chops

Day 17

Breakfast-Sweet Potato with Cranberries

Lunch- Juicy & Flaky Salmon

Dinner- Simple & Delicious Pork Chops

Day 18

Breakfast-Cheese Omelet

Lunch- Flavorful Chicken Fajitas

Dinner- Air fryer Pork ribs

Day 19

Breakfast-Zucchini Egg Muffins

Lunch- Quick & Juicy Tilapia

Dinner- Dijon Lamb Chops

Day 20

Breakfast-Greek Egg Muffins

Lunch- Easy BBQ Chicken

Dinner- Brined Pork Chops

Day 21

Breakfast-Crispy Breakfast Potatoes

Lunch- Flavors Blackened Salmon

Dinner- Marinated Pork Chops

Day 22

Breakfast-Herb Egg Breakfast Muffins

Lunch- Healthy Greek Chicken

Dinner- Tender & Juicy Pork Chops

Day 23

Breakfast-Cheese Egg Bake

Lunch- Asian Salmon

Dinner- Flavorful Steak Bites

Day 24

Breakfast-Italian Egg Muffins

Lunch- Sesame Chicken

Dinner- Sweet & Juicy Pork Chops

Day 25

Breakfast-Kale Egg Muffins

Lunch- Moist & Crisp Cod

Dinner- Steak Bites

Day 26

Breakfast-Savory & Crispy Hash Browns

Lunch- Tender & Flavorful Chicken Breast

Dinner- Air Fryer Perfect Steak

Day 27

Breakfast-Zucchini Egg Muffins

Lunch- Lemon Butter Cod

Dinner- Delicious Steak Fajitas

Day 28

Breakfast-Kale Egg Muffins

Lunch- Cajun Chicken Thighs

Dinner- Juicy Pork Chops

Day 29

Breakfast- Greek Egg Muffins

Lunch- Spicy Salmon Fillets

Dinner- Sweet & Spicy Pork Chops

Day 30

Breakfast- Cheese Omelet

Lunch- Simple Adobo Chicken

Dinner- Simple & Juicy Pork Chops

Conclusion

The Ultrean air fryer is all in one cooking appliances available in the market. It is a versatile cooking device capable to perform different cooking tasks like air fry, roasting, grilling, and baking into single cooking appliances. You never need to purchase a separate appliance for each function. The Ultrean air fryer is very simple to use anyone can easily operate this appliance. It is capable to cook almost all types of healthy and delicious dishes. The air fryer comes with a 4-quart cooking capacity which is large enough for a small family to cook their daily meal.

This cookbook contains healthy and delicious air fried recipes comes from different categories like breakfast, poultry, beef, lamb, pork, seafood, fish, vegetables, side dishes, appetizers, snacks, and desserts. The recipes written in this book are unique and written into an easily understandable form. All the recipes start with their preparation and cooking time followed by step-by-step cooking instructions. Each recipe written in this cookbook ends with their nutritional value information.

www.ingramcontent.com/pod-product-compliance
Lightning Source LLC
Chambersburg PA
CBHW081346070526
44578CB00005B/746